Honoring Aging Parents

Honoring Aging Parents

How to Grow Up When Mom and Dad Grow Old

Klaus Dannenberg and Bruce Black

ISBN 13: 9781948484497
Published by Clovercroft Publishing
Franklin, Tennessee

Contents

Authors

Klaus Dannenberg is a retired engineering executive with an aerospace and information technology emphasis. During the prime of his career, shortly after becoming an empty nester, he and his wife spent twelve years taking care of his wife's parents when they were no longer able to live independently and were gradually losing their capabilities. One had Alzheimer's, and the other had congestive heart failure. Additionally, after his mother passed away, his father remarried a woman several decades younger, creating additional and challenging stresses to overcome.

Bruce Black has been a practicing minister for more than thirty-five years who recently began counseling in gerontology, both for the aging as well as their caregivers. Shortly after he and his wife became empty nesters, his mother-in-law suffered a stroke, from which she never recovered. He and his wife were thrust into maximum caregiving responsibilities for her and her spouse, while knowing virtually nothing about the subject.

The authors' combined experiences span a wide range of common caregiving situations, each having complementary experiences to the other. Despite preconceived ideas of the great burden and difficulties of caregiving, both the authors and their spouses found contentment and satisfaction while providing comfort to their parents. Their suggestions and advice are practical and comforting for those who find themselves in similar circumstances with little or no preparation.

Acknowledgments

There are many who come to mind who deserve thanks for sharing with us their experiences, feelings, frustrations, and joys; for sharing our burdens through our difficult caregiving times; and for contributing to the preparation of this book, the first for both of us. But primarily, we want to thank God for independently making both of us aware of a richer and fuller meaning of the fifth commandment, to honor our parents. It is also through our Christian fellowship that we know each other and discovered our natural inclination toward working together on this project.

We obviously want to thank our parents and in-laws. They have blessed us and our families with a lifetime of care, support, and love. We often teared up when we were trying to put poignant memories into words, writing vignettes and summaries of past events. The preparation of this book brought back recollections of many past events and feelings, putting them all in perspective well after their occurrence. We hope and pray this book honors each of them.

We also want to thank our children, Lindsay, Jessica, Kerry, and Chris, and their spouses. Thanks for your support in the concept and preparation of this book. Your encouragement was invaluable. Writing this book made us want to make your lives easier as you go forward and honor your aging parents. We love you all.

Specifically, we also want to thank Chris for her marketing support and book-cover design and Lisa Castello, our content editor. Totally by accident but fortuitously, Lisa was also our target audience—that is, an adult child with aging parents recently in transition. On occasion, she stopped work to attend to her parents' needs because the content she was editing pricked her heart and conscience, causing her to take action. Whenever she related those events to us, we gained confidence that we were on the right track.

Finally, we want to thank our wives, Betty and Jeanette, who have borne so many of the burdens of caregiving while maintaining our homes and families. They are respectively God's greatest gift to each of us—best friend, counselor, mentor, supporter, and lover. Our lives continue to get better because of them. Each of us looks forward to growing old with them, knowing that the best is still ahead of us as John Lennon penned in the words of the song "Grow Old With Me."

Honor your father and mother. Then you will live a long, full life in the land the Lord your God is giving you.

—Exodus 20:12

Chapter 1

Introduction

This is not a typical "how-to" book in that it doesn't explain in a step-by-step manner how to take care of your parents as they age. It also isn't a knowledgeable treatise on the philosophy of caring for aging parents written by gerontology experts. Then what exactly is it? It is a collection of useful experiences, insights, and suggestions that we learned the hard way, by taking care of our parents as they slowly lost their independence and needed our help. As authors, we are not experts or researchers on aging, financial or legal planners, physicians, social workers, or psychologists. Rather, we are rank amateurs—normal individuals who stumbled into the challenges of caring for our aging parents when we were completely unprepared. This is a book that we wish we'd had.

When we first realized that our parents needed help and needed it right away, we were overwhelmed and quickly began looking for help. Despite the advice we sought and received from well-meaning friends, acquaintances, and specialists, we both had uncomfortable, lingering feelings of helplessness. Though we felt completely unprepared, we had to make decisions and take action fast.

Through the next combined twenty-five years of helping our aging parents, we've had countless conversations with other caregivers, as well as with elder-law lawyers, physicians, social workers, and various consultants on aging. We've also read whatever information we could find on different aspects of caregiving, often at the height of our need (and confusion). Still, we've often wondered what we could have done to better prepare ourselves. More recently, we've wondered what we could do to lessen this burden for our own children (who are all now adults) when they become caregivers for us. Surprisingly, that is still not as clear as we'd prefer. We'd love to have a formula or a comprehensive checklist. Instead, we offer our own lessons learned, subtle insights, or good ideas of what we should have done, all presented as anecdotal examples and followed by some conclusions. If that approach appeals to you, please read on.

Sooner or later, all adults who live long enough will experience the effects of aging. Even the best-intentioned families too often do not plan for aging and the inevitable migration toward a dependence on others. There are lots of self-help books telling us that we don't need to age and that we should stay forever young. That's a pretty appealing concept, for sure, but it ignores the reality. We all age and lose at least some of our capabilities over time. Worse yet, there is not "a solution" that fits everybody. Every family situation is different in regard to finances, relationships, emotions, physical health and well-being, cognitive understanding, and willingness to help out. Many of our parents plan for their own passing. That is definitely important. But what happens when they slowly become feeble and unable to care for themselves? This frequent reality needs to be given some thought and adequate planning.

In our experience, geriatric experts have a wealth of technical knowledge. We surely need to hear and comprehend it, but their advice is often rendered in an objective and clinical manner. That dispassionate advice is often hard to grasp and doesn't feel like it addresses our specific problems. So as authors, we set out to discuss and unravel our own personal situations, pinpointing a few things that could have prepared us more fully for decision-making about our parents' aging process:

1) **Insights into alternatives and their consequences**

    We needed a greater understanding about the consequences of our decisions and actions, not only on our parents but also on our own families and ourselves. For example, we never anticipated that well-intentioned decisions about where to locate our parents might not work out as well as we'd hoped. We also thought downsizing only happened once after retirement. Little did we realize that it was a continuing part of a new lifestyle that was repeated over and over again. Financially, too many times we tried to save a few hundred dollars only to find out in six months or a year that those decisions cost us a few thousand dollars. Some real-life anecdotal examples would have cautioned us against many of these mistakes.

2) **Understanding the long-term nature of caregiving**

    It took time to understand the long-term nature of caregiving as each of our parents aged with different degrees of grace and rapidity. Each time we thought we had addressed the immediate situation as well as possible, it soon morphed into a new situation that required more awareness and consideration of another new set of alternatives. Each time this happened, we had to pull ourselves together again and move on. All too slowly, we recognized that this was a part of life—our new reality. Sadly, we were certainly not the first to encounter these situations. A little advice could have saved us a lot of anxiety and possibly even motivated us to take a different approach.

3) **Awareness of natural emotions and frustrations**

As we shared experiences with each other and with friends and family in similar situations, we were startled to learn of the many similarities, no matter what the situations happened to be. Our friends reacted in the same erroneous ways that we did when they became new caregivers. It would have been helpful to understand the range of emotions encountered by others and how they responded. Some common reactions were the following:

*   I thought I was the only one in this situation! Because my friends had not dealt with it in a visible way, I didn't have anyone to talk to about it.
*   I wish I had some emotional support and guidance for the path ahead. I did not have confidence in the decisions and actions I was taking.
*   I was embarrassed by the thoughts and feelings I had about caring for my parents.
*   I owe my parents so much, yet I felt so helpless and inadequate when it came to knowing what to do or even what the choices were.

Because of the awkwardness, we never talked about these topics. In hindsight, we really regret that we didn't do so.

Sometimes, we just needed a hug! Some measure of comfort and direction can come from a greater understanding and awareness about the challenges of aging and caregiving, even when we don't have all the answers yet. Understanding the landscape to come may be the "hug" needed during emotional stress.

The Companion's Perspective

In the introduction to his book *Reflections on the Psalms*, C. S. Lewis explains that two students are often better able to help one another understand a difficult topic than their instructor may be. The instructor mastered the subject so long ago that he has likely forgotten the challenges involved in understanding the issues. Those issues are no longer real to the instructor, who sees the subject in an entirely different light than the students anticipating difficulties that the students have not yet begun to comprehend and ignoring their immediate daily challenges. The students, however, come at the problem from the same vantage point and, therefore, are often better able to help each other. They recognize the emotions involved and can offer the encouraging "hug" needed to bear down and continue, even if only to take the next immediate step.

Similarly, as rank amateurs in the world of caregiving, we are not aware of all the studies and research that have gone into understanding the various aspects of gerontology. All we know is that we encountered many evolving challenges in the few decades of dealing with our own parents' aging.

With that perspective in mind, our purpose for this book is to

1) *stimulate a greater awareness* of what's ahead for many of us as our parents age;

2) *encourage others to start discussions* about caregiving alternatives early enough to make informed decisions; and

3) *improve the quality of life* of all those involved—parents, children (whether grown or still at home), siblings, and extended families.

The Expert's Rightful Place

This book is not intended to in any way replace the professional help needed for medical, legal, or financial issues. On the contrary, we frequently suggest when to get this help and encourage the active pursuit of helpful advice. As with much of the material included in this book, our suggestions are usually the result of our own mistakes. In trying to be "penny wise," we wound up being "pound foolish" in the choices we made about professional help. Those mistakes were often expensive—financially and emotionally. When avoiding decisions on difficult issues because we were unprepared, we often created worse scenarios down the road. If only we had gained some timely awareness and insights, maybe we could have avoided some of those costly and emotional errors. We hope this book helps you avoid some of those mistakes.

The Stories Ahead

In discussions with other caregivers, we have found an amazing consistency in many of the challenges encountered. Furthermore, we have been comforted to share similarities in the paths taken. Each situation described in the following chapters is a real-life experience that has been lived by one of us or another caregiver known to us. We describe these situations in short vignettes—that is, in stories using aliases to protect the feelings and identities of those involved. Each story describes the situation; how it was dealt with; and, in hindsight, what was learned or how we might have dealt with it differently. We hope these stories will help you

1) *anticipate and prepare* both yourselves and your parents for caregiving challenges;
2) *transition* your parents from independent living to dependent living;
3) *downsize* into a sustainable caregiving environment; and
4) *cope* with a continuing and frustrating loss of capabilities and independence as your parents age.

Many of these stories are disturbing. Many are humorous. Some are poignant. Several are sweet. Simply put, that's life! Although the observant reader will recognize several families who appear multiple times, there is no need to keep up with them. Each story describes a stand-alone situation intended to illustrate one example with no additional background needed.

Honor Your Father and Mother?

Our book is written from a Christian perspective, but we recognize that most religions value the wisdom and the role of the elderly. In our younger days, we thought the fifth commandment, to honor your father and mother (Exod. 20:12), was intended for rebellious and smart-aleck kids. Little did we realize then that the promise associated with that commandment ("that you may live long in the land the Lord your God is giving you") is most meaningful when we have become mature adults. No matter how old we are, our father and mother always retain their roles as our parents. Therefore we should honor them, as well as their memories and legacies, through our entire lives, even after they pass away.

Jesus's statement of the golden rule is also directly applicable. When he said, "Do to others as you would have them do to you" in Matthew 7:12 and Luke 6:31, it applies to everyone we encounter, including our parents. But the fifth commandment adds the dimension of honor when dealing with our parents. As our parents become unable to care for themselves (and especially if they have different ideas about their care than we do), we are still instructed to honor them. In facing differences of opinion, a good self-test for us has been to ask the question, "Am I honoring my parents like God thinks I should?" That perspective colors everything we do when providing care for our aging parents. If we are not doing so, then we immediately feel guilt. But over time, that guilt can turn into grace if we are able to learn from our own mistakes (and hopefully those of others too). Often, it's only in the rearview mirror that we can truly see how blessed we've been by the process of honoring our father and mother.

Remember the teenage boy who thought his father knew nothing? Twenty years later, after marriage, a career, fatherhood, and other aspects of maturation, that young man was amazed at how much his old man had learned. Similarly, it's hard to explain the understanding and wisdom gained as well as the spiritual, emotional, and intellectual growth attained by assisting your parents as they navigate their way through their loss of capabilities, their transition to dependence on you (since we assume you must care since you are reading these words), and their final years. Of course, there will be times when tempers will flare and opinions will differ. But we achieve meaningful blessings of love, patience, kindness, and other fruits of the spirit (Gal. 5:22, 23) when we encounter life's trials and detours in the caregiving process.

Chapter 2

Preparing to Take Care of Parents

Facing Facts: Recognizing When Mom and Dad Need Help

Senior Moments or What?

Most of the time, the signs are all around us, but we simply don't see the evidence. Even if we do see it, we don't understand it. That's because for all our lives, our parents have been the decision-makers, the experts, the ones with all the experience and expertise—they are the "go-to" people for us. When we notice a little slip in some area of daily living, we overlook it and think, "That's cute—a senior moment." And, in fact, that assumption is often true. So we ignore the incident and forget about it.

Other times we quickly become impatient when our parents "forget" what we told them just a few minutes ago or when they can't find groceries in the store they've been going to for decades. With an edge in our voice, we'll say something like, "Come on! You know that." Then they'll be too embarrassed to discuss it, and we may dismiss it as just a random incident. However, when there begin to be a lot of these senior moments and they occur in multiple areas, it's time to pay attention. In addition, we may also have hurt their feelings with our tone of voice and our attitude. So an increased awareness is definitely worthwhile. Let's look at a few personal examples.

The Baker-Not So Much Anymore

Beth noticed that when her mother Alice was in her mid seventies, she was no longer able to make chocolate-chip cookies. Alice had been a gifted baker all of her life, and her cookies were a family favorite. The first time Beth noticed that her mother's recipe failed, she wrote it off as an honest mistake, and everyone laughed about it. But then it happened again. And again! Eventually, Beth and her husband recognized that Alice was losing her ability to bake cookies. Since Beth's family lived about ten hours away by car and only visited once or twice a year, this shift was not an obvious daily occurrence. During visits, the family often ate out, so mistakes at home often went undetected. But one day after several months, Beth said, "Boy, it would sure be great to have some biscuits." Alice said she didn't have the ingredients on hand. At some long overdue point in time, it occurred to the rest of the family that Alice was no longer cooking much. That's when Beth seriously started taking note of Alice's capabilities. The early signs had been there all along, but Alice did an excellent job of working around her deficiencies, and fooled herself, her husband, and Beth for several years.

Making Change

Tom showed signs of losing key mental capabilities when he could no longer make change. His daughter and her husband Curt did not notice that he was challenged in this area for quite a while since it wasn't creating any problems. One day, when they were making some minor purchases at the store, Curt noticed that Tom probably had ten dollars in change in his pocket—just bunches and bunches of quarters, nickels, dimes, and pennies. Curt joked that Tom would tear out his pockets if he didn't get rid of some of it. They both laughed, but shortly afterward, when Tom pulled out his billfold to pay for another small item with a bill, Curt suggested, "Why don't you pay for that with some of that change in your pocket?" Flustered, Tom held out a handful of change and said, "OK then, you do it." Only then did it occur to Curt that Tom could no longer make change.

Soon after that, Curt had an opportunity to look at Tom's checkbook register and discovered that it was thousands of dollars out of balance. After Curt and his wife discussed it, they decided to offer to balance Tom's checkbook for him. He accepted right away and was greatly relieved. Soon after that, Curt also offered to do Tom's tax returns since he had a computer program that would make the process easy. Curt and his wife soon took over all of Tom's finances. Only then did they realize that Tom had probably been struggling for several years but was too embarrassed to say anything about it.

Playing Hide-and-Seek

Alice was always a bit distrustful of others, but not noticeably so to most people. As she aged, she began hiding her purse, even at home, "for safekeeping." After a while, she couldn't find her purse when she wanted it. Whenever her daughter, Beth, went anywhere with her, they had to find her purse. As this hide-and-seek continued, Alice would cry and get upset, even to the point of yelling and slamming drawers, until the purse was found. She was excellent at hiding her purse, so it often took Beth, her husband, and Alice's husband fifteen to thirty minutes to find it. After talking with other caregivers, Beth discovered that this was actually a pretty common occurrence.

Other families experienced similar behaviors such as hiding eyeglasses or clothing so they wouldn't be "stolen." In another situation, Mary hid apples. She was offered apples in a caregiving environment a couple of times a day since it was a good, healthy treat. She usually accepted them but then, rather than eat them, she frequently hid them in her closet, drawers, or wherever she could in her room. Eventually, Mary's caregiver had to spend at least one day each week playing "find the apples," so they wouldn't rot and smell and make a mess.

Minding the Meds

A few years after retirement, Fred was taking a total of ten medicines. He took six of them once a day, but not all were taken at the same time of day, and four of them were taken twice a day. So twice daily Fred took out his basket of medicines, read the instructions on every single bottle, and then took out and assembled a handful of medicines to take. His daughter Jane thought it was cute, but she was also amazed. She asked him how he was able to keep up with all of them. He sighed and said it was hard. His comment surprised her. So Jane bought him a five-dollar weekly medicine minder with twenty-eight compartments in it (a compartment for his medicines for breakfast, lunch, dinner, and bedtime for every day of the week).

For weeks, Jane thought the problem was solved. But then she noticed that when Fred ate a late breakfast, he would sometimes take his breakfast and lunch medicines all at the same time—at lunch. Or if he skipped a meal, he also skipped his medicines. Other times, he doubled up and took two doses at once. So the medicine minder really didn't solve the problem. Even worse, by taking his medications incorrectly, Fred created significant chemical imbalances that caused him to feel bad and often made him worse.[1]

Reading the Fine Print

Carl was always looking out for his grandkids, so his son George was not surprised that he opened a custodial college savings account for each of them. But one day, Carl proudly told his son about an investment he had just obtained that "guaranteed" an exceptional rate of return. Since Carl always had been a smart investor and was an engineer, George trusted his father's judgment on monetary issues. Besides, he didn't want to challenge Carl's investments or interest in the grandkids.

Some months later, George read the investment material at his leisure and was shocked to find that it was a deferred-income-type investment—the principal could not be withdrawn without penalty until the grandchildren were fifty-nine and a half. The money set aside would be several decades too late to help with college expenses! When George asked about it, Carl said he hadn't noticed that clause. Either the sales agent didn't explain it to him very well,

---

1 Several pharmacists have indicated anecdotally that a major problem with aging seniors is not taking medicines as prescribed, creating severe medical imbalances in their frail bodies and resulting in unanticipated consequences. That also impacts additional treatment by their physicians since, of course, they assume that the prescribed medicines are being taken as intended.

or he didn't understand it. This was the first time George had serious concerns about Carl's diminishing capabilities, but it certainly wouldn't be the last.

Freshening Up

Rose noticed that her mother, Mary, frequently didn't smell as "fresh as a daisy," even after she indicated that she had bathed. Soon Rose learned that Mary's "bath" was only a sponge bath, and she often wore pantyhose and underwear for several days in a row, not realizing that she kept putting the same ones back on. When Rose suggested that she might need assistance in bathing and dressing, Mary took it as a huge insult and reacted with indignation. But after Rose suggested it was special pampering, Mary let her help her. Soon Mary seemed to be completely happy to be helped in bathing.

Around the same time, Mary also started wearing ill-matched clothing even though she had always dressed neatly. Sometimes she even had her clothes on backward or inside out, or she wore her shoes (even heels) on the wrong feet at church. Through a trial-and-error process, Rose learned that framing suggestions like, "Let me show you the latest trend that people are wearing now," worked much better than pointing out the errors.

Monitoring the Signs

These examples illustrate a few of the "slips" in daily living that can be early indicators of the impact of the aging process on our parents' behavior. These signs are often easy to miss or overlook, especially if we don't interact with our parents regularly due to lack of proximity. They can include minor incidents of forgetfulness, loss of capabilities, erosion of lifelong skills, or poor judgment.

**A single incident can indeed be
written off as a senior moment.
But even then, it's a good time
to start observing
a bit more carefully and watching
for any emerging patterns.**

My mother exhibited these symptoms well before any of our other parents, so neither I, nor my wife, understood what was happening. I was not only clueless but also completely insensitive to the process. I often joked with my mother about these incidents (and surely hurt her feelings without thinking). With our other parents, these changes began to occur about ten years later. By that time, we had learned more about the aging process and had observed others dealing with the phenomena, so we were more attuned to the changes and their implications. Then we could take the first important step—acceptance of the changes and loss of capabilities that come with aging. At that point, we could begin to consider the myriad of alternatives in caregiving as well as how to broach this touchy subject with our loved ones. Though it was painful, we realized we could not ignore the signs. In hindsight, we should have acted in my mother's case a few years earlier. But even though the process took time, at least we started discussing alternatives. More on that in the next sections.

Financial Assessment: Avoiding Expensive Mistakes

Assessing the Situation

Much has been written about financial planning for our retirement, but not nearly as much advice addresses financial planning for the care of our aging parents. As previously mentioned, this book focuses more on emotional and mental preparation for becoming a caregiver. But financial preparation should not be overlooked. It is key to almost any viable solution, and mistakes are seldom recoverable. Our own experience is that many serious mistakes come in increments of a thousand dollars or more. Several were even in ten-thousand-dollar increments! We made several of them. This is unnecessary and completely unaffordable!

The major financial issues that caregivers (or potential caregivers) should consider are

* their parents' personal financial resources;
* their private retirement and long-term care plans; and
* any government-sponsored plans for which they may be eligible.

Assessing each of these will help determine exactly what finances and assistance can be counted on. This sounds obvious, but the resources available in retirement are being used up and are generally not replaceable. They are perishable. In direct contrast, while our parents are still working, they can still generate income to correct mistakes and replace wasted opportunities. After retirement, that's no longer true for most of them. To plan effectively as caregivers, we need to anticipate our parents' financial needs. After we accept the responsibility of caregiving at any level, we must answer these questions:

* What are the savings? How accessible are they, and by whom?
* What retirement income is available, and when? Will it be adjusted for inflation, or is it a fixed amount (which is usually the case)?
* What other income is available? (Possibilities could include rental income, royalties, or residual commissions from sales.)
* Is any insurance coverage included with the retirement plans?
* What is the expected social-security income for each parent?
* What level of Medicare premiums will they be required to pay? (Remember, the amount is income-dependent.)
* What outstanding debts do your parents have? A home mortgage? One or more car loans? Credit-card debt?
* Do your parents have any special medical or physical requirements that need to be considered?
* If so, are any insurance payouts available to help offset these requirements? This could include payouts from long-term care or disability insurance, for example.
* What are their expenses, routine or otherwise? (These could include utilities, insurance premiums, taxes, and much more.)
* Do your parents' physical, emotional, and mental conditions require immediate professional care (usually in some type of facility providing care)? Or is that down the road, if needed?
* How much are you (and your siblings, if any) willing to underwrite the financial needs for your parents, if necessary?

Eventually, you will need to do this financial planning in detail. But initially, some rough estimates will suffice. Even if you do not have this information readily available, you will be surprised at your ability to generate good guesses if you take a little time to do some research.

**Do not consider alternatives that
are totally unaffordable.
That unnecessarily hinders the
assessment process.
Alternatively, if resources are
sufficient, there is no
reason to scrimp on little things
that make life easier.**

Sketching a rough budget is a good place to start, even before you have the initial talk with your parents about their care. Remember that your parents were already making ends meet at some level before you got involved, so you certainly will not be starting from scratch. Details can be worked out as things evolve.

Understanding Retirement Income

Financial planning for your parents is no different than developing a budget for yourself, but you'll probably have to familiarize yourself with the elements of retirement income. Typically, these include social-security income; expense offsets from Medicare and Medicaid; any retirement income from qualified plans, such as employer's retirement, IRAs, or 401(k) or 403(b) plans; annuities; and the use of savings to generate regular income. Most of us have spent our entire lives putting funds into these plans, so they have been an expense. Now, we will be taking money out of them without putting additional funds into them. And that change in perspective is a *big* one!

A typical breakdown of retirement income and support includes:

* **Social Security and Retirement Plans**
  In these key income elements, there is usually a "normal" retirement date with a fixed amount of monthly income paid out. Earlier-than-normal retirement reduces that amount, while later-than-normal retirement increases that amount. Countless books have been written on strategies for maximizing these income streams in more situations than we will ever encounter, depending on marital status, total financial status, age, and expected lifetime of the individuals (i.e., the mortality tables), among other factors. A little research will reveal many options and give you good insight into the alternatives.

* **Savings**
  The other key element is the amount of your parents' savings. In this case, the primary additional consideration in income planning is the tolerance for risk. That determines asset allocation into equities, fixed-income instruments, and cash.

As we frequently recommend, find and use a financial advisor. Objective insights are highly valuable. A few hundred dollars spent up front is well worthwhile.

At a minimum, try to involve a financial advisor specializing in elder care to provide an independent, third-party sounding board for your own ideas. A competent elder-care financial planner will also be up-to-date and fully conversant on local laws and requirements for qualification for various governmental support plans.

* **Medicare and Medicaid Plans**

Though these health plans are the other primary difference in retirement financial planning, many of us are not familiar with them at all.

Considering these major questions and how they relate to health care can help you avoid expensive mistakes.

A Big Question-When Do We Sell the House?

When they were preparing to take care of Barb's parents, Ken and Barb were correctly more concerned about their health and their emotional state than their financial state. Having decided to move Barb's parents into their home in another state, Ken and Barb did not want additional entanglements and ties. So when Barb's father decided to sell their house, Ken thought that was a good thing, eliminating responsibilities and liabilities in another state. Plus, that would give them a nice surplus of cash to invest and save for a rainy day.

But selling the house did not create a cash surplus, as expected, because Ken and Barb didn't know that Medicaid allows both a residence and an automobile to be exempted from the assets that are considered to qualify for Medicaid. However, once the residence is sold and converted to cash, then all the cash must be spent before an individual can qualify for Medicaid. Over the next few years, all of the cash from the house (and more) was spent on assisted-living care for Barb's parents before they were eligible for Medicaid assistance.

This turned out to be a six-figure mistake that certainly could have been avoided. If Ken and Barb had maintained and rented the house, they would have faced additional responsibilities and expenses, but they would have eventually inherited the house, and then sold it. An early discussion with an elder-law attorney would have made them aware of this situation. The accumulated value of the house would have more than offset the costs of the attorney, the rental management, and other expenses.

The governing laws for these programs are written with good intentions: to prevent last-minute actions intended to avoid taxes; to ensure that assets are not simply transferred to relatives and friends to quickly qualify for government subsidies and assistance; and to avoid fraud, both by the elderly as well as by those interacting with the elderly (which, unfortunately, often includes family).

As with other aspects of financial planning, some of the governing laws are federal ones, and some are state (and those laws are different for every one of the fifty states). To complicate things even more, these laws change on a regular basis. So again, it isn't feasible to address all of these in a reasonable and complete manner in this book. To qualify for assistance while avoiding any last-minute transfer of assets, action usually needs to be taken several years in advance. That means that assets have to be transferred multiple years prior to consideration for government assistance.

Accounting Decisions-Cash versus Accrual

When preparing the documentation for Ted to qualify for Medicaid, his son-in-law learned that the government evaluated the eligibility for Medicaid on a cash basis (and *not* on an accrual basis) at the beginning of every month. The maximum assets allowed to qualify were in the low four figures, but on a cash basis (that is, whatever the bank statement showed as the account value at the close of business after crediting any deposits and debiting, as well as withdrawals or checks cashed).

Having just written a check to pay off a large doctor's bill (in the low four figures), Ted's own personal check register showed a balance of only a few hundred dollars at the first of the month, an amount small enough to qualify. But the recent check that was written to the doctor did not clear the bank account by the end of the month. It cleared a few days afterward, as shown on the bank statement.

Therefore, in following the state law, the social worker correctly declared Ted ineligible for Medicaid, since the bank balance was well over a thousand dollars above the maximum asset allowance. So Ted's family had to absorb another month's expenses in a nursing home before qualifying for Medicaid the following month. If he had written the large check a week earlier or if he had requested that the check recipient cash it right away and prior to the end of the month, Ted would have qualified one month sooner.

This mistake was worth one month's nursing-home expense—a five-figure mistake. And sadly, again, it was totally avoidable. But it would have required paying attention to accounting terms and monitoring resources at a level of detail that they normally wouldn't consider. Another expensive lesson learned.

Power of Attorney-Who Signs What?

Often, one parent handles all the finances, and the other is clueless about them. When the parent who handles the finances becomes ill (even for a short time, like a few weeks) or becomes unable to handle the finances, who will take over? Sometimes the other parent can do it. With joint checking accounts, that's no problem (at least from a legal perspective). But knowing who to pay and understanding any budgetary constraints still makes this a challenge.

When Jean began handling her parents' finances, she obtained a durable power of attorney for both of her parents and was added to their checking accounts as a third signer. This simplified the ability to handle many financial transactions. As her parents neared the end of their lives and were close to exhausting their resources, she began to get their affairs in order to qualify them for Medicaid.

The Medicaid practices where they lived (which are different in every state) required that her parents separate their assets. As a result, although they had always had one joint checking account, they now needed two. Further, the local Medicaid practices also required additional separation of their daily finances from a "burial account" that would be used to pay their burial expenses when they passed away. This was totally understandable and a good practice overall. It assured that enough resources were available for required end-of-life expenses. But it meant an additional account for each of them. So as they neared the exhaustion of all their assets, the Medicaid regulations drove Jean's parents to having four bank accounts, even though they were out of money and had lived for over sixty years of adulthood with only one checking account.

Not questioning these practices, but simply executing them, Jean went about establishing the extra accounts. Her father's was easy. Although he was in poor physical health, he was still of sound mind and signed the paperwork (with Jean as co-owner of the accounts). But when Jean tried to open new accounts for her mother, it was another story entirely. Jean's mother had Alzheimer's and did not understand what was going on at all. But Jean was told by the bank officials that she could not use the established durable power of attorney to open a new account. When she asked, "Why not?" she was shown that the legal language of the power of attorney empowered her to conduct "all the financial and legal practices that her mother normally and customarily conducted as a part of her life." But, she was told, neither of her parents customarily opened bank accounts, since they had only had one account throughout their lives! In disbelief, Jean asked how to handle the situation. The bank official said her mother would have to sign in person. Again, in disbelief, she brought her mother in, had her "make her mark" (which was a scrawled X), and opened the account. In further research after the fact, Jean discovered that many banks customarily do not accept powers of attorney and are not required to do so.

Despite this incident, the power of attorney was extremely useful for many other activities. But it illustrates the type of surprises that were encountered on a regular basis. In hindsight, this would have been something an elder-law attorney should have caught. But Jean's parents had developed the power of attorney about ten years prior to this situation, and it wasn't written in anticipation of caregiving responsibilities. If Jean had consulted an elder-law attorney in advance, hopefully this could have been addressed.

Next Steps

Once you roughly understand the overall financial situation, consult with an elder-care planner or attorney as far in advance as is feasible. Even at the earliest point in the caregiving process, several hours of professional consultation is worthwhile.

The attorney will probably also recommend developing new powers of attorney for both financial and health-care matters as soon as you become deeply involved in caring for your parents. In addition, an attorney will usually recommend new wills, living wills, or maybe even a trust. All of these are excellent recommendations and should be addressed with your parents (once that awkward discussion is held).

Early on, the primary information to be gleaned from the elder-law attorney is insight into laws and requirements that you need to be aware of as you begin executing caregiving responsibilities since they will have a substantial impact on the finances. Most parents will not have received legal counsel about these, since they are typically frugal and will not want to spend the money. This was our own experience, as well as that of many other caregivers we have known.

Assessing the Alternatives: Needs, Opportunities, and Affordability

Navigating the Maze of Needs

After deciding that your parents need some help and becoming somewhat familiar with their financial capabilities and needs, you are ready to broach one of the most difficult discussions that you'll ever have as they age. As you prepare to have "the talk" with your parents for the first time, be prepared to consider the broad spectrum of needs. What kind of help is best-suited for your parents right now? Ideally this should be your assessment first, not theirs. Most of our parents are independent, and they want to continue to be independent. Therefore, they will often assume that they don't need any help. That discussion can be addressed more directly later. But to avoid being surprised with alternatives that you had not considered at all, try to answer the following questions as objectively as possible:

*   Do your parents need help with their *normal activities* because of the natural consequences of aging? This includes things like cooking, laundry, housekeeping, yard maintenance, shopping, making and keeping doctor's appointments, and handling money.
*   Do they need help with *personal daily needs* that would embarrass them to admit? This can include assistance with things we probably never anticipated helping our parents with: eating and dressing, and, oh yes, bathing, toileting, and continence.
*   Or are they already in a *worst-case* situation with some type of cognitive impairment or medical incapacity?

After assessing their needs, your options boil down to three broad categories:

* <u>Do-it-Yourself</u>—You and your family provide the help, whether in your home or in your parents' home.
* <u>Hired In-Home Help</u>—You and your family find responsible and affordable help to enable your parents to continue living in their own home.
* <u>Assisted Living</u>—Their level of needs and your own limitations dictate some level of assisted-living care or a nursing home.

If a worst-case scenario already exists when you first become involved, the choices will be pretty limited. But fortunately, this is not usually the place most of us begin.

By growing in awareness of your parents' capabilities and not avoiding these painful discussions, most caregivers can start slowly and easily with do-it-yourself assistance, and then move gradually into other areas, as needed.

Let's look briefly at the various levels.

<u>Do-it-Yourself</u>: This is an easy way for most of us to start. You can have a big impact simply by being aware of little situations where it is obvious that something is going undone or noticing when your parents are having a hard time with things. You don't need to make a big deal out of it. By noticing that the yard needs to be cleaned up or by helping out with household chores, you can start the process. Sometimes, you don't even need their agreement. In my own case, my parents had a large two-acre yard. Every time we visited, I sent our kids out to pick up branches and minor debris in the yard. I could see that it made a difference to my mom and dad, and they never once said, "Oh, you don't need to do that." Unfortunately, at that time, I was not aware of their growing fragility, so I didn't take the opportunity to expand this assistance much. We all helped with cooking and cleanup afterward, but we could have done so much more.

Other assistance that makes a big difference is volunteering to help make doctors' appointments or even to take them to the doctor or to pick up prescriptions. Also, volunteering to take them shopping is almost always welcomed, whether it's getting groceries, shopping for events like birthdays and holidays, or simply accompanying them to the mall to get some needed new clothes. It's surprising how helpful these little things can be. But the greater value is also that it provides extra time together when you can ask, "Is there anything else I can help you with? How about getting a little something for Dad (or Mom)?" The first time you're in this situation, the answer may be, "No thanks," but it won't be long before they welcome the opportunity to spend time together for such purposes. At some point, they may also suggest (though perhaps reluctantly at first) ways you might help that you haven't thought about.

More personal things, like handling money, will probably require a greater awareness and a bit more tact than the easier tasks. But a situation will eventually occur when you can sense their frustration or uncertainty. That's the time to ask, "How can I help with that?" Again, the first time they will probably decline politely. But once they know that you are aware, and are genuinely interested and available, it won't be long until they welcome some assistance and accompaniment. It may initially be as an advisor or as a sounding board to discuss things and get an objective opinion. After they see that you won't simply criticize their way of doing things, it's only a matter of time until they seek the next level of do-it-yourself help.

Hired Help: This is where the options increase exponentially. But that's a good thing because you will surely be able to find affordable help in some useful areas. Finding regular household help or yard maintenance is an easy place to start. A monthly or weekly visit may even be welcomed for the more tedious or challenging tasks. Once a level of acceptance and confidence has been established, it's an easy step to increase the frequency of this type of assistance. But you should prepare yourself for some initial grumbling about how it's not affordable or how the quality of the help and the actual results are not as good as doing it themselves. You may have to try several helpers before your parents slowly realize (even though they may not admit it to you) that the help is needed and good enough to be useful. If you don't need this step, that's great. But realistically, this resistance stage may last months or even years.

Even more challenging is getting your parents to accept elder day care. This will include the following, but will likely include other areas as well:

Day-care centers—in which your parents are taken to a central location where they and others needing care are offered various forms of entertainment, meals, assistance with taking medications, and social opportunities while under the supervision of trained social workers and nurses.

In-home companion care—where responsible and capable adults come into the home to provide companionship, prepare minor meals, and possibly provide other assistance while maintaining a knowledgeable awareness and observation of the situation. Companions can call you and others for assistance if needed. This service can often be provided by friends and relatives if they are available, have the right temperament, and are willing to do so. Your parents' acceptance of strangers versus friends is hard to predict and will vary on an individual basis. So it's always useful to try a variety of approaches.

Most of these alternatives have direct parallels in childcare for taking care of young children. As a result, sooner or later your parents may say, "I'm not a baby, and I don't need babysitters!" For sure, they are not babies. They have years of adult experiences, and they have developed opinions and preferences over decades. So in many ways, it's harder to find help that they will accept. But for the same reasons that small children need sitters, your parents also need responsible, capable, and observant companions to help them. Just as it was a trial-and-error process when your kids were small to find competent babysitters or day care, it will also take time to find acceptable alternatives that meet the needs of your parents.

Assisted-Living and Nursing Homes—This is the option that no one ever wants until there are no other workable choices. The primary alternatives are assisted-living centers, rehabilitation centers, and nursing homes.

Assisted-living centers recognize that individuals often still want to do as much as possible for themselves and can, in fact, do quite a bit. But they need help with some things like dressing, bathing, toileting, and other functions. If one parent is capable of caring for him or herself but not of taking care of a spouse who needs help, assisted living is often an excellent alternative. Assisted-living centers also provide companionship with other elders as well as various entertainment options. Most of these centers provide several levels of increasing assistance (but at a commensurate rate of increased costs). Finding and entering a center with these options is an excellent way of providing care that can be ramped up when the need arises without a major change in environment.

Rehabilitation centers are needed (and consequently accepted more readily) when a parent has had an injury or medical procedure that needs exercise followed by supervised care. Almost any time someone has had surgery for breaks, for joint or organ replacement, or for major repair work, a period of time in a rehab center will usually be prescribed by the attending physician. One major positive aspect about rehab centers is that everyone expects the stay to last for only a short time, so there is usually much less resistance and grumbling about going to a rehab center than there might be for another type of care. And if the rehab needs to be extended or morphs into more dependent care, the patient is already in the facility and does not need to be uprooted and moved.

Finally, nursing homes are for individuals who need constant care. They are often bedridden. Many nursing homes are affiliated with or even directly attached to rehab centers, so if rehabilitation is not working or additional steps are needed, a transfer from one section of the facility to another is a simple and logical step. If a nursing home is needed right away, there usually isn't a lot of discussion needed or even possible about alternatives. Though everyone wants to avoid that alternative, once it becomes necessary (usually by doctor's orders), then we must find a viable facility and make the best of it.

Transitioning One Step at a Time

Harriet retired from the state-hospital housekeeping department at the mandatory age of seventy. She was a divorced, single mom with a great work ethic who had raised two boys, despite having only an elementary-school education. Shortly before her ninetieth birthday, she fell and broke her hip. A year later, she broke her wrist when she fell while trying to start her lawn mower. She managed to start the mower, cut the grass, and put the mower away. When her wrist swelled and became discolored, she wrote it off as a nuisance.

Since her two sons each lived a day's drive away in different directions, they had no idea what had happened. Fortunately, a friend noticed the swollen and discolored wrist and took Harriet to the local hospital where the physician diagnosed her broken wrist. The friend called Harriet's sons, who quickly came to take care of her.

While Harriet recovered, her sons, Don and Seth, found someone to cut her grass. They also arranged to have an elder day-care service provide female companions to stay with Harriet during the day, giving Don and Seth some peace of mind. However, the elder day-care service didn't last long. They were supposed to send invoices to the sons so that Harriet wouldn't see them and protest. But when they mistakenly sent the monthly bill to Harriet, she was outraged by the amount (even though she wasn't paying for it herself and it was actually reasonable). So she fired them and sent any future companions home when they appeared at her door.

At this point, the sons visited Harriet together, sat down with her, and told her that the next time she injured herself in any way, they would be forced to move her into an assisted-living facility near one of them. Although they both appreciated her desire to live in her own home, her independence and fragility had evolved into a vicious cycle of injury, hospital stay, and then rehab. Of course, she protested vigorously, but they left her with that ultimatum while they researched alternatives for longer-term solutions.

The final incident occurred when Harriet was ninety-three. She had noticed a tree root coming up in her lawn. She got down on her knees with her hatchet and started chopping the tree root out. She severely injured her back, which required a lengthy hospital stay and more than a month of rehab. While she was in rehab, her sons (both of whom had retired at this point) assessed their alternatives and decided she should live near Don, the youngest, in a nice, affordable facility they had located.

A couple of days prior to her release from rehab, the oldest son, Seth, flew down and picked up a rental truck while Don drove up to move her. On the day of her release, they brought her home and helped her pack her clothing and a few items of furniture she wanted to keep. Surprisingly, she put up little resistance. The move took place with little emotional toll on anyone.

**The process of assessing alternatives often
occurs over a period of time
(even up to a few years)
between multiple triggering incidents.**

Too often, the first time that we even face the need to start this process, we write it off as a one-time incident and don't really plan ahead. Don and Seth were wise to begin serious discussions with their mother and their search for assisted-living options after Harriet had her first incident. The interim measures they tried gave them time to collaborate on longer-term solutions, which will usually be needed sooner or later.

Journeying toward Appropriate Care

Once Nancy's dad, Ted, recognized that he and his wife Betty could no longer live by themselves, he called and asked for help. Ted had congestive heart failure while Betty had Alzheimer's that was just beginning to show itself. Although it was challenging, Ted had maintained their house and yard in a small town for several years. But when Betty's Alzheimer's began to show, he was unable to ensure her safety and take care of their home. Physically, Betty was strong and healthy, but Ted's strength was ebbing even though his mental capabilities were still excellent.

Since Nancy's youngest child had just graduated from college and moved out, she and her husband had room in their home to accommodate her parents right away. At this point, there was not much to assess in the way of alternatives. They accepted Ted and Betty into their home and worked it out.

This arrangement worked well for about a year, with Nancy taking care of most daily functions for Ted and Betty (such as preparing meals, housecleaning, and laundry) as well as helping them with scheduling and shuttling them to doctor's appointments when necessary. Over time, Nancy noticed that they also needed help with financial tasks, and she took those over too. When Nancy and her husband wanted some time for themselves, Ted was able to take care of things for a few hours or even a day or two.

However, within a short period, Nancy's parents began to miss the companionship of their peers. Nancy began researching various types of in-home and day-care assistance. Through trial-and-error, the day-care solution was eliminated, but in-home companion care worked out nicely. Nancy identified several paid companions as well as one or two of her friends who would sit with her parents in her home, play games with them, and prepare meals.

This second arrangement (increased attention and care, but living in Nancy's home) worked well for several years until Betty became increasingly agitated and difficult to handle, both for Ted and Nancy. So Nancy began the next stage of seriously assessing alternatives. Assisted living was significantly more expensive but also relieved Nancy and her family of providing daily care. After consideration of costs, facility and staff capabilities, and distance from Nancy's home, an assisted-living facility was selected for Ted and Betty. Although Nancy expected some resistance, it didn't materialize. Ted recognized and accepted the need while Betty, whose Alzheimer's had advanced, did not really seem to understand what was going on.

They were unable to take their furniture with them, so the unavoidable next stage of downsizing occurred quickly.

Nancy visited her parents several times a week and brought them home for meals and family events. She also took them to church, outside activities, and doctors' appointments, and generally still provided her parents with regular caring attention.

That arrangement lasted for about two years until Nancy's dad was hospitalized. With hospitalization, he could no longer take care of Betty. Therefore Nancy again conducted additional research, looking for places where both parents could be close to one another, since they could no longer stay together. She found a convenient Alzheimer's facility for her mother as well as an attached nursing home for her dad.

This lasted for another two years until her dad passed away. At that time, Nancy was aware of a closer nursing home where she could place her mother. Since Betty was unaware of her surroundings by this time, her final move went smoothly and without any resistance. She stayed at this nursing home until she passed away several years later.

This example illustrates the full spectrum of needs and solutions. Over a ten-year period, Nancy's caregiving ranged from do-it-yourself and various types of assistance before culminating in assisted-living and nursing-home alternatives. While she hadn't imagined the possibility or the need for nursing-home care initially, she grew into those alternatives and became aware of options as her parents' needs changed.

**Changes in the spectrum of care evolve naturally
as we encounter and understand
the needs at hand.**

"It Takes a Village..."

The old African proverb, "It takes a village to raise a child" can also apply to caregiving for an aging parent. As we begin to understand our parents' needs and choices, most of us are overwhelmed and need access to different kinds of help, more than we ever imagined. With the gradual aging of the baby boomers, caregiving alternatives are constantly evolving.

One new concept, called "the Village," has emerged to help aging people stay in their homes. The concept originated in the Beacon Hill neighborhood of Boston in 2002, when a group of residents founded a nonprofit organization called Beacon Hill Village.[2]

The Beacon Hill Village was formed to facilitate access to the services that often force older Americans to give up their homes and move to retirement facilities. Since this first village was formed, the idea has spread throughout the United States. Within a few short years, the village movement has grown to more than seventy villages throughout the United States with another seventy in the planning stages.

Villages are membership-driven, grass-roots organizations that, through both volunteers and paid staff, coordinate access to affordable services including transportation, health and wellness programs, home repairs, social and educational activities, and other day-to-day needs, enabling individuals to remain connected to their community throughout the aging process. Villages customize, personalize, and humanize a living environment and lifestyle. The village movement honors people's interest in staying in their own homes and has the benefit of creating a deeper and stronger sense of community.

---

2 www.beaconhillvillage.org

The village neighborhood organization is led by a volunteer board usually augmented by one or two paid employees. Members from the community pay an annual fee (currently the US average fee is $600) to their neighborhood village in return for services such as transportation, yard work, household chores, and shopping. The village doesn't provide services; it serves as a liaison between members and service providers. Typically the services come from volunteers who live in the same neighborhood as the village members. Villages also provide lists of approved home-maintenance contractors, many of whom offer discounts to village members. Through this structure, the village hopes to offer a menu of assistance that members would receive in a retirement community and allows them to stay in their current home and community.

The national resource for villages is the Village-to-Village Network. Their website lists existing villages and the communities they serve throughout the United States. The website also provides a tool kit for people interested in starting a village in a new community.

The authors first learned of the village concept while living in the Washington, DC, area, and continue to be impressed by it. Currently, the National Capital area leads the nation in village communities with forty villages that are either operational or in development. The idea of the village is one in which our parents were raised: neighbors helping neighbors. If your parents are typical elders, they will want to "age in place" and remain in their home for as long as possible. A village helps that happen.[3]

---

3 To learn more, visit the Village-to-Village Network's website: www.vtvnetwork. org. For a better sense of what villages offer, refer to Tara Bahrampour, Through a Growing Number of Senior Villages in the DC Area Aging in Place Becomes Easier, *Washington Post*, February 6, 2014, www.washingtonpost.com/local/through-a-growing-number-of-senior-villages-in-the-dc-area-aging-in-place-becomes-easier/2014/02/06/e51fc660-7fbf-11e3-9556-4a4bf7bcbd84_story.html

Now that Preparation is Complete

Admittedly, if you have researched all the topics addressed here, you will have done a *lot* of work. But in all likelihood, some of the options will not be affordable. Some will not be acceptable. Some may sound good, but good practical examples may not be available in your area. Nevertheless, the foundation for your current and future caregiving needs has been established. As your parents' needs change, as financial capabilities evolve, and as new options become available, you will most assuredly revisit the spectrum of alternatives again.

Having done some research, you are now ready to have that daunting first discussion with your parents. With a little forethought and a bit of good fortune, you may be able to drift into parts of that discussion while still assessing the alternatives. The gradual transition is great if you can pull it off. Regardless, it's time to get started.

Tough Conversations with Parents about Aging

Preparing for "the Talk"

After facing facts and assessing viable care options and the financ-es to handle them, at some point we must have "the Talk" with our parents. That is definitely easier said than done! If you have ever attempted to talk to your aging parents about the realities facing them as they age, you are aware of just how off-limits this subject is for most people. Not only do you have to get up the nerve to bring up the subject, but your parents also have to be willing to engage in the discussion. "Active denial" describes most parents' initial reac-tions fairly well.

The reality is that they have likely already discussed this between themselves and with their friends. But they are embarrassed and vul-nerable and probably not ready to discuss it yet. When that is their reaction, don't push it. Step back gracefully with a comment like, "I know this is uncomfortable, but when you're ready, we really do need to talk about these things. None of us is getting any younger, and I'd like to hear your ideas while we explore this together." Then at a future opportunity, try once again to start the discussion when it comes up naturally. Each time the subject arises, it will be a bit less frightening. Sooner or later, the right opportunity will present itself.

**It often takes multiple attempts
to start the conversation
before any meaningful progress is made.**

But if the subject is continuously deferred, reality will eventually catch up, and you will wish you had broached the subject earlier, no matter how difficult it is to talk about. When a significant fall or infirmity arises, there won't be time to make deliberate decisions after loving, coherent, and cooperative discussion. So without being insistent or rude, return to the subject whenever opportunities arise—from friends' situations, from fictional stories in a novel or the movies, from human-interest stories in the papers or on the televised media, from legislative impacts on social security or Medicare, or from any of a host of other things that may stimulate this discussion. With our general population aging as the baby boomers move steadily into retirement, there are countless anecdotal examples that are given wide attention on a daily basis. Use any of these to initiate "the Talk" with your parents.

A Picture of Denial

Ben was driving with his mom and dad through picturesque Malibu Canyon, enjoying the scenery. His dad was sitting to Ben's right in the passenger seat, and his mom was in the back seat. Ten minutes into the trip, Ben boldly decided to change the subject from what they had at McDonald's for breakfast and made this declarative statement. "We need to start talking about your plans for growing older."

His dad immediately chimed in. "Son, you don't need to worry. We've made all the arrangements for our funerals. All the details are taken care of."

Ben, a minister, replied, "Great, Dad. But I'm not talking about your funeral plans. I've helped with several hundred funerals. I'm comfortable with making those arrangements. I'm talking about your life plans as you age. There are a lot more decisions to be made about aging than where you want your ashes scattered."

This statement was met with silence for the rest of the drive, everyone having their own thoughts. No one really wants to have this talk, and many react with denial, even if only at first.

When the Bottom Fell Out

At age eighty-four, Jane's mother, Nell, was a poster woman for health and aging. She had remarried fifteen years before. Together she and her husband Cecil seemed to be ageless. In recent years, Cecil had shown some signs of the early onset of Alzheimer's disease, but even in battling that, the twosome seemed to not skip a beat. Then without warning, the bottom fell out. Nell had a series of strokes that left her a shell of her former self. These strokes took her speech, much of her cognitive abilities, and her physical strength and stability. Since Nell was left speechless from her strokes, Jane realized all too late how little she knew about Nell's desires and wishes.

Sadly, this is a common occurrence when the future caregiver, with little or no warning, is instantly thrust into a full-time caregiving role with little understanding of what is desired, what is possible, and what is available.

Surviving as a Widower

Ken's father, Carl, had survived his wife's death after a long period of her immobility. Carl decided to sell the house where he and his wife had lived for thirty-five years because the yard was about two acres of wooded property, and he could no longer take care of it. Carl bought another house and did so without any discussion with Ken.

Though not surprised when Carl bought a condominium with no yard, Ken was stunned to learn that it had three stories with stairs that would become harder each year for Carl to navigate as he aged. When Ken raised that issue, Carl told him, "I am in good health, and, in any case, I installed an elevator so I wouldn't have to handle the stairs daily."

Ken decided he really needed to talk with Carl about his future needs but didn't take advantage of the opportunity presented by the sale and the resulting move. Ken assumed he could have this discussion with Carl later, after he had done some research and was better prepared for it.

As Carl grieved the loss of his wife, Ken didn't understand the natural loneliness that Carl felt. Consequently, Ken was shocked once again when Carl remarried with only about a month's notice. As a result, the opportunity for Ken to talk with Carl slipped by for well over five years. During that time, Carl changed his will several times and relocated to yet another house. All of Carl's actions were surprises and sometimes didn't appear to be in his best interests. Much of this may have been avoided if Ken had taken advantage of any of several natural opportunities to have "the Talk."

Moving into Assisted Living

One of the hardest things to do is to move parents out of their home of many years. Doug's parents lived in a bi-level house for more than thirty-five years. In a bi-level, the entry is on the lower floor, but most of the living space is on the second level. When Doug's dad had a stroke at seventy-four, his reduced mobility made it a struggle to get up and down the stairs. Since his left side was strong, and the stair handrail was on the left side, going up was feasible and worked out pretty well—slow, but stable. Going down was another matter. He couldn't maintain his balance if he went down facing forward. So, he began going downstairs backward, holding the handrail with his strong side. It seemed to work, but it was scary to watch. To make things worse, with his reduced mobility, he also began to gain weight. No surprise! Walking was hard. And while he still managed to drive, when he was home, he tended to sit around. As his weight went up, the trip downstairs became ever more frightening.

The condition of Doug's dad, along with his mother's increasing difficulty with walking, finally compelled Doug to bring up the subject of moving. When Doug told his siblings that he thought their parents needed to move, the response he received was, "Yeah, right." His concerns were ignored, and he received no support. This issue was complicated because Doug's oldest brother lived with their parents at the time. Therefore, if the parents moved, Doug's brother would also have to find a new place to live.

After letting it sink in with his siblings, Doug brought it up to his mom and dad. He initiated the conversation gently at first. "Have you guys ever thought about selling the house and moving into a retirement facility?" There wasn't much response. Doug brought it up again each time he saw them, which was every week or two.

Finally, they agreed. In hindsight, their hesitancy was largely driven by the challenges of the actual move. After it was all done,

Doug's dad asked him how he had organized and executed the move, because he couldn't imagine how to actually do it. His dad was more of an idea guy and not as much of a doer. Trying to envision how to do it had been the biggest impediment. After the move, Doug's parents were safer and more content, and interacted with others to a much greater degree.

Why Is This So Hard?

Having the initial conversation with our parents about the impact of their aging is one of the most difficult conversations we will ever have. And the follow-up discussions about their desires and the choices that need to be made are equally as hard. That's true for a number of reasons.

First, we live in a time when many people, including most of our parents, often see age as a handicap rather than an honored achievement. Many aging adults have taken Rod Stewart's ballad, "Forever Young," as their generational standard. They deny the facts and are reluctant to discuss the subject of aging. Let's face it. One of the worst insults in today's youth-oriented world is to be offered a senior discount when you are still underage!

A second reason it's so tough for some of us to talk to our parents about their aging is that we often still feel like kids when it comes to them. As young people, we found stability, assurance, and comfort in our parents' vitality, energy, drive, work ethic, and youthfulness, whether in play, in carrying out tasks around the house, or in guiding our future with advice (though usually unwanted at the time). Now a few short decades later, the impact of their aging often causes adult children to go into denial because it flies in the face of the childhood perception of them that we still hold deep in our heart. When you add the reality that, at some point, our parents will die and be taken from us, our own fear and avoidance can make us totally unwilling to talk to them about their aging process. We just don't want to face it.

A third factor that complicates talking to our parents is simply the complexity of the aging process. To borrow from Churchill's view of the new Russia, "...it is a riddle, wrapped in a mystery, inside an enigma." Churchill's description also fits the aging process well. As we struggle to keep up and stay afloat in our own lives, we know little, if anything, about the financial, physical, emotional, and spiritual elements of aging. We tell ourselves that we will figure out the social-security system and Medicare A, B, C, and D later. We might drive by a nursing home or assisted-living facility or see an article about active adult communities or continuing care retirement communities. We are somewhat reassured that those options are available, but we really have no clue about what they do, what they cost, what the differences are, or how to help someone become a resident of any of the available choices. We tell ourselves that we will deal with that when the need arises, not realizing that we will usually have precious little time to absorb, assess, and evaluate the alternatives.

Finally, when we see the signs of aging in our parents, we can easily become immobilized. We may enter their home and notice that the volume of the television is at deafening levels. Mom and Dad are always in sweaters, and their home thermostat is superglued at some unreasonably warm temperature. We may see that they move with a shuffle rather than walk. The content of their conversations seems to bounce between their constipation and their diarrhea. They take handfuls of pills every day, and when Dad tries to explain what each pill is for, we intentionally zone him out in fear that he is going to explain the purpose of the *blue* pill.

Here's the bottom line.

Mom and Dad don't want to grow old.
You don't want Mom and Dad to grow old.
The world of growing old is a mind-numbing mystery.
You see the signs of aging but can't interpret them (or refuse to).
As a result, you are overwhelmed and speechless.

How Do We Approach it?

The answer to the age-old question, "How do you eat an elephant?" can be applied to our dilemma. Of course, the answer is, "One bite at a time." Just like you don't eat an elephant in one bite, the same is true when it comes to talking with parents about aging. When you finally do, you might be so emotionally wound up that you've prepared dozens of questions and think you'll get answers to all of them in one sitting. And since you are likely uptight about it, you may have a scowl on your face the whole time and be determined to lock the door and hold them hostage until they answer all the questions to your satisfaction. But with that approach, even rubber hoses and bright lights probably won't get your parents to open up about their thoughts and ideas about aging.

Instead, touchy topics need to be taken on a "one bite at a time" basis, visited and revisited again and again. There is almost a "dance-like" tempo and tone to them. As with any emotional topic, when you talk to your parents about their aging, it's best to approach it with care and calm, dealing with the non-emotional aspects first.

**The first conversation will not get all the
answers that you want and need,
but it will open the door to future
conversations. You can trust that they
are thinking about it after you leave. The
next time may be more productive.**

The key to making this work is to look for opportunities, and then take advantage of them. This requires an ongoing awareness and yields the best results.

An approach that brings other rewards is to ask your parents to share memories about their parents as they aged. Ask them, "How did your parents handle aging? How did you, as adult children, handle your parent's aging?" This should be safe ground to start the discussion. You can also ask what things they wish they had done differently. These discussions will open doors and provide opportunities to learn more about your parents' histories and their hopes and desires.

Another approach is to casually ask your parents how they are doing, while watching for more details than you normally would. Ask for the specifics of the pills that you see lined up on the kitchen or bathroom counter (and you can even be impressed by the *blue* pill's functions). Ask how you can help with chores around the house. Offer to go with them to their doctor's appointments or to pick them up for church or to run them to the store. As you assist them out of the chair or when you provide a stabilizing shoulder for them to lean on, calmly ask how they are managing with their aches and pains. These are usually areas that we ignore or don't want to know about. Just asking will often result in surprised looks. But showing a continued interest in these matters will be appreciated and lead to greater insight and continuing discussions.

Slowly but intentionally build bridges to conversations about aging. Find ways to become more integrated into the current reality of your parents' lives.

As you participate in their aging process, it will become easier to go deeper into a meaningful dialogue with them. Realize that no one (including you) wants to be unexpectedly slapped in the face with the big questions of life. We are all more likely to talk about important things with people we love and trust. Further, we are more prone to have these discussions in the midst of life's daily rhythms.

After getting more engaged with your parents and their aging, you may find yourself sitting with them in their home when you sense the opportunity to go deeper. You calmly begin to talk.

"This house is pretty big now that all the kids are gone. I know it takes a lot of effort and money to maintain. Those stairs must be getting tough to deal with. Mom and Dad, what are your thoughts about keeping and maintaining the house? How long do you think you want to stay here? And what do you think are the next steps?"

Then sit quietly and listen. Believe me, the questions about taking care of the yard and handling the stairs are ones that virtually all aging seniors discuss and worry about on a regular basis. There's an excellent chance that your parents are as nervous and anxious about growing old as you are. They are facing a new and rapidly changing reality, all the while holding onto their self-image of being self-sufficient. But as hard as they may try to deny it, part of them usually knows that they can't do what they used to do.

Many parents still view their adult children as people they take care of, not the other way around. From their perspective, no matter how old they get, a parent's role is always to support and provide for the children. The thought of asking for help from one of the kids is as foreign to them as using a phone to take a picture. So it is imperative that you help them see by your involvement in their daily routine that you care about them and that you welcome and embrace the changes that aging is bringing into their lives.

Your ability to get your parents to open up
about aging is linked to your willingness to be
a vital part of your parent's current reality.

If you are on the inside of your parents' current life when you ask them,

"Mom and Dad, what are your thoughts about keeping and maintaining the house?"

And they answer,

"We're staying here forever. There are no problems with maintenance or money. We're handling everything."

You will see the practical challenges they're facing because of your involvement in their lives. Even if they're in denial, you can offer solutions, one at a time. You'll know they are trying to show some bluster. But they'll know that you know they are simply kidding themselves.

If you were an outsider to their lives, you would have to accept them at their word or start an argument based on what you think, rather than what you know. But as you become more invested in their lives, the conversation can proceed a bit differently. You can respond with something like the following:

"Wow, you're handling everything yourselves? That's impressive since I have a hard time myself with home maintenance. It's hard for me to get on a ladder and look at the roof or to go up in the attic (or down in the basement) to store and retrieve stuff. And the stairs are killing my knees! Are you *really* sure you're handling everything? I know how hard it is, and I'm willing to help."

"I notice that your air conditioning will need to be replaced in eighteen months, and the roof needs to be replaced this year."

"What about this yard? I'm glad to mow it, but trimming, weeding, and winterizing is too much for me, much less for the two of you. I know that I can't give it all the attention it needs."

"Maybe we can share a maid service for cleaning up: dusting, vacuuming, and cleaning the bathrooms. That's a lot of work."

"And that's not to mention the touch-up painting and minor plumbing work that always seems to need attention."

"Any house is a challenge to maintain. I know because of my own, and I've been helping you, so I see your needs too."

"Are you sure you don't want to talk a bit about easing your workload or even about reconsidering your future living arrangements?"

When you are a part of a person's life, you can hear the bluster but not be fooled by it. So you stay calm and patient, summon your most respectful tone, and reframe your questions and concerns about their current reality. And even if you don't make the breakthrough the first time you broach the subject, you've laid the groundwork. Sooner or later, they will start the discussion.

If you don't live close to your parents, the process of getting involved in their current reality takes more creativity and collaboration with others.

You'll need to talk frequently to your parents and speak with them about their day-to-day friends, activities, and schedules. You'll need to take a keen interest in their lives and gently, but intentionally tease out of them what they now face as they move through life. As you begin to build a bridge of discussion about the bigger issues of aging, start slowly and on topics that are not emotionally charged for your parents or for you.

For example, if they mention to you a friend who has fallen ill or who has passed away, use this as an opportunity to take the conversation to a different level. Calmly ask,

"Mom, I'm so sorry to hear about Mabel's passing. Is there anything I can do for her family? Please give me the details, and I'll be sure to send flowers. But Mom, how do you feel about this? I know you and Mabel were close friends for many years. What's going on inside of you, now that she's gone?"

An obvious opportunity we will face with half of our parents is helping them through the loss of their spouses. The time immediately afterward would be too painful. But sometime soon, when they have come to grips with their spouses' passing, and they may be involved in settling the estate, the opportunity will present itself to ask, "What about your future?" Some downsizing will probably be going on, even if only disposing of their spouses' things that are of no sentimental value. Some financial decisions will have to be made, even if only notifying social security, Medicare, or pension plans. In addition to taking care of these necessary actions, this is a chance to show your care and concern and then take the opportunity to discuss the surviving parent's future.

By paying attention to your parents' actions and needs, you'll have a better chance to know their friends, their interests, and their struggles. Just as importantly, you will show your parents how much you care.

Summarizing: Steps to Starting the Conversation

1. *Recognize and release childhood perceptions of your parents.* Whatever your childhood perceptions of your parents were, they need to be reframed in current reality. We dealt with this earlier in the section "Facing Facts."

2. *Get educated about the aging process.*
   Though aging can be a daunting subject, many available resources offer insights and ideas into its impact and how to deal with it. Many of these were addressed in the sections about financial assessment and assessing the alternatives.

3. *Get involved in your parents' current reality.*
   When someone feels uneasy about a situation, a natural tendency is to avoid it. When it comes to your parents and their aging—don't! Embrace it. Understanding their needs is critical to finding viable solutions, as discussed in the following section.

4. *Start talking about non-emotional aspects of aging.*
   Most people talk about "big issues" in their own time, at their own pace, with the people they trust and love. Your parents are no different. So start the conversation with less emotional, noncontroversial subjects.

5. *Calmly and strategically ask the bigger questions.*
   Take advantage of opportunities to ask questions about the more important and emotional issues. We will discuss these issues in the next section of this book.

Understanding What Care Is (and Isn't) Needed-and When

What's Needed Now? Later?

After facing facts and realizing that our parents need some help, most people feel overwhelmed. Tremendously overwhelmed! But don't panic and assume that Mom and Dad will need a full-time nursing home and that the costs will bankrupt you. This extreme situation is seldom the case.

> **Just like it was when raising our children, our parents' life changes come gradually and allow us time to prepare. We take each new step while we are learning about the process of caregiving.**

Children don't morph from birth into full-grown adults instantly. Neither do independent adults immediately need full-time care on a 24-7 basis. Of course, that can sometimes happen in unusually extreme cases. But usually, our aging parents have an evolving spectrum of needs that can be met by an array of alternatives. Years ago, our children progressed along an ever-growing set of capabilities, learning and doing more over time as they grew and matured. Similarly, our aging parents regress along that same spectrum, only they are losing their capabilities as they age.

However, once you recognize that help is needed, their need will regularly and nearly always require greater care in the next phase. So there is usually time to adapt; to study, anticipate, and learn how to help; and to decide what's affordable in time, attention, and financial support. Numerous services and options are available at various price points. Determining which of these will work and which are acceptable to you and your parents will be a process of trial and error. No matter how much we study the situation, the human frailties and emotions involved cannot be fully anticipated.

The following examples illustrate some typical circumstances and the responses that may be encountered.

Cry for Help

Tim and Alice were living on their own, a full day's drive from their daughter Beth. They seemed to be doing quite well on their own. Beth and her family visited once or twice a year and talked with them regularly by phone. Alice had early signs of Alzheimer's. Although Beth thought it was not very advanced, it definitely had a noticeable impact. In contrast, Tim had congestive heart failure and was not in great physical health. But he seemed to be taking care of their daily needs pretty well. Tim was also fiercely independent, never wanting to depend on anyone else for anything. But Alice, due to her Alzheimer's, could be persistent, asking the same question over and over and not understanding or recalling the answers.

One evening when Alice persisted in her questioning and Tim couldn't take it anymore, he called Beth and told her that he could no longer take care of Alice by himself. He needed help. Alice was also getting out of the house, becoming confused, and then getting lost somewhere in the neighborhood. Tim just couldn't keep up with her. Months earlier, Beth had told her dad to call if he found that he couldn't manage, so she wasn't completely surprised, although the timing was unexpected (but then, isn't it always?).

Once Beth and her husband fully understood the situation, they had to do something—quickly. The immediate decision required live-in help or Tim and Alice's relocation, either close to Beth or in a caregiving facility near their home. There was no need to "talk them into it" since Tim had called for help. So in this case, Tim proactively asked Beth to collaborate in planning and managing their future, an arrangement that worked well for several years.

The Move-In

Since Beth's children were living on their own, she had room in her house for Tim and Alice. Tim quickly disposed of most of their belongings, and Beth relocated her parents to live with her. In hindsight (see the section about financial assessment) and from a financial perspective, Beth erred in allowing Tim to dispose of their stuff too quickly, specifically in selling their house.

But the relocation and move-in went better and easier than expected. Both Tim and Alice were healthy enough to negotiate the stairs of Beth's two-story house every day. They could dress and feed themselves. Beth took them to doctors' appointments and handled most of their everyday needs. Tim was still able to care for Alice for several years, so Beth and her family could also plan some time to themselves.

The Day-Care Solution?

Beth arranged a bedroom for Tim and Alice and converted a second small bedroom into a den with their furniture. This allowed them some additional independence while living in her home. But all they did was watch TV, so they quickly became restless. After doing some research, Beth found a senior day-care facility about fifteen minutes away that seemed nice and well-managed. Beth could drop them off several times a week or even daily, depending on their needs. It seemed like a perfect solution to keep Tim and Alice active with people their age while still monitored by a knowledgeable staff. Although Tim was not excited about this solution, he recognized and supported Beth's need for a break from Alice's constant demands for attention.

The first visit to the facility went well. Tim and Alice seemed excited about the prospect of new friends and activities. But after the first visit, Alice decided she didn't like it. She complained that everybody there was old and feeble, just waiting to die, and the food was terrible. In hindsight, Beth probably could have better prepared Alice with some extra time and effort. But since Beth was new to caregiving and didn't understand how to help Alice with the transition, senior day care became unworkable within a few months. It was a chore to get Alice into the car to go and a bigger chore to get her out of the car at the day-care center. More than once, Beth was called by the center to come pick them up early.

This solution didn't work for Beth because she was new to the process and didn't spend the necessary time preparing her parents. That was an important lesson learned. Spending some time pre-evaluating the day-care activities and, if necessary, locating a different facility that would allow Alice to do things that interested her could have made this a more appealing alternative.

The Day-Care Solution Part Two: In-Home Care

Soon after Tim and Alice rebelled against the senior day-care approach, Beth discovered Senior Companion Care, essentially an in-home sitting service for seniors. Sitters would come into her home, prepare simple meals (like sandwiches or microwaved meals), and provide companionship while Beth and her husband had an evening out or ran errands that required them to be out of the house for several hours.

As was the case when Beth used babysitters for her kids, there were good ones and bad ones. The good ones really cared and enjoyed spending time with Tim and Alice. They played games, talked with them, and gave them genuine, excellent care. They learned about their lives and even gave them small Christmas and birthday gifts. The best sitters did not do it for the income but because they truly cared about people and wanted to help. One companion even stayed in touch with Beth and her family many years after this phase had passed. But even the "bad" companions were fine, overall. If Tim and Alice did not care for a sitter, they simply stayed in their den and watched TV while the companion provided meals and left them alone. Beth felt assured that her parents were safe and their needs were taken care of while she was gone, so she didn't have to worry about them getting into dangerous situations. That peace of mind was well worth the fees.

Taking Stock-What Is (and Isn't) Needed

This phase is critically important and is different for every situation since there are a countless number of variables.

* Is care needed for one parent or two?
* Is physical assistance required, assistance in cognitive understanding, or both? Whatever level and types of care are needed now, more of both will probably be needed soon in the future.
* To what degree can the parents still contribute—physically, financially, emotionally, or cognitively? The more they can

understand and help, the better they will feel about the situation, themselves, and the caregiver.

* Do you still have children at home? That will significantly impact your availability and definitely needs to be considered.

At this evaluation stage, we are not yet assessing resources and solutions. We are simply trying to identify and define the needs.

Installing grab bars in the bathrooms or ramps at the stairs is a different solution than hiring care for a parent with dementia or Alzheimer's. Helping your parents while also caring for young children is much more challenging than doing it without children around.

The big questions (referred to earlier) revolve around the following areas:

* Living arrangements
* Medical concerns
* Driving and transportation
* Financial planning and management
* Knowledgeable and prudent decision-making

The key issues are briefly addressed here. It can be difficult to determine exactly what is needed. Deciding on solutions is even more difficult, but to agree with your parents on what's needed is the critically important first step.

Living arrangements: When can your parents no longer continue in their present living situation? Alternatives could range from living with other family members or hiring in-home, live-in assistance to the extreme of relocating to professionally staffed fa-cilities. Decide what your parent must be able to do to live without assistance. Collaborate with other close family members on a plan to continually assess each parent's health progress and household needs.

Medical concerns: What do your parents want to do when one (or both) of them dies or becomes immobilized, critically ill, injured, or unable to perform the daily activities of life? Together, decide on a specific course of action and what measures should be taken in each of these scenarios.

Driving and transportation: Agree upon the capabilities needed for parents to continue to drive. Who will make the deci-sion about when they should no longer drive? Collaborate on a plan for their transportation needs should they reach a point where they can no longer drive.

Financial planning and management: What does it cost for your parents to maintain their current lifestyle and needs? How much money do your parents currently have; how and where is their money invested; and how long can they continue living like they are? Do they have a budget? Are they keeping to it? Can they physically pay their bills? When they are unable to handle their fi-nances, what are their wishes? Work with your parents to establish a financial plan that will include social security, retirement, and other investment income as well as their monthly living expenses and the cost of extra things like travel, vacation, and gifts.

Decisions: Billy Graham once said, "All my life I've been taught how to die, but no one ever taught me how to grow old." It is the rare parent or person who can successfully face the challenges of aging alone. So be sure to talk with your parents about who they want to be involved as they make decisions about their future. Ask them, "Which friends and family members do you want in your inner circle of advisors as you make decisions about where to live and your health, mobility, finances, and estate?"

Bette Davis was once quoted as saying, "Aging isn't for sissies." She was right! It takes intentional planning by the caregiver to garner the trust needed to talk about subjects that are volatile to both parents and adult children. It requires the ability to control emotions and move beyond perceptions held over a lifetime. It requires perseverance and patience to move deliberately through a minefield of explosive subjects coupled with the endurance to visit and revisit topics that are too important to be avoided. And it takes a lot of love in the form of selfless commitment and investment in the current lives of your mom and dad. Growing old isn't for sissies—and neither is caring for your elderly parents.

Dealing with Siblings: Where Is Everybody When You Need Them?

Can Everybody Contribute?

Sibling dynamics play an important and emotional role in dealing with aging parents. The denials and potential roadblocks of either a parent or frustrated siblings can be difficult for adult children who are trying to help with meaningful caregiving. Siblings often aren't willing or prepared to play any role in their parents' care, whether physical, financial, or emotional. Whether it's fair or not, daughters are usually more actively involved than sons. In an August 8, 2014 *Washington Post* article, Fredrick Kunkle reports that women step up to provide care for their aging parents more than twice as often as men, citing a study by Princeton doctoral candidate Angelina Grigoryeva titled, "When Gender Trumps Everything: The Division of Parent Care among Siblings."

Kunkle states, "The new research found that in families with children of both sexes, the gender of the child is the single biggest factor in determining who will provide care for the aging parent: Daughters will increase the time they spend with an elderly parent to compensate for sons who reduce their involvement, effectively ceding the responsibility to their sisters."[4]

Other findings suggest that one sibling typically leads the way in caring for aging parents. Researcher Ingrid Connidis, PhD, from the University of Western Ontario discovered,

---

4 www.washingtonpost.com/national/health-science/daughters-provide-twice-as-much-care-for-aging-parents-than-sons-do-study-finds/2014/08/19/4b30cade-279b-11e4-86ca-6f03cbd15c1a_story.html

In 43% of U.S. families and 41% of Canadian families, one sibling has the responsibility for providing most or all of the care for Mom or Dad, according to a survey of family caregivers. In only 2% of families in the U.S. and 3% in Canada did the siblings split the caregiving responsibility equally.[5]

The rest of the siblings seem content to take a secondary role (or even a ringside seat) in care and communication with their aging parents. That usually causes frustration and resentment in the life of the sibling who carries the load of connecting, communicating, and caring for the aging mom and dad. Let's look at some examples.

Recognizing the Need to Work Together

While vacationing, eighty-two-year-old Dorothy fell in the hotel parking lot. She was in enormous pain that radiated from her left knee and hip. George, her husband of sixty-four years, rushed her to the hospital for tests and emergency treatment. The fall caused a hairline fracture in her left hip socket. George called his oldest child Candy (a daughter, of course) to tell her about the fall and asked her to contact her three adult siblings and share the status and test results. Candy immediately texted her siblings (all adults fifty years old or older) about their mom's hospitalization.

The oldest son, Bob, called Candy for a more detailed update. During the conversation, they remembered this was their mother's second serious fall in three years and also recalled the car wreck she caused a couple of years earlier. Both wondered aloud if this was a developing pattern. If so, should something be said to Mom

5 www.caregiverstress.com/wp-content/uploads/2011/08/The-50-50-Rule-Helping-Siblings-Overcome-Conflict.pdf

and Dad to make sure they were aware of this emerging "trend" of accidents? Or would this be interfering?

Fortunately, the two of them decided to work together and organized the support of their other siblings. But too frequently, it takes a serious mishap before siblings start talking about their parents' need for support.

Whose Side Are You On?

Multiple siblings usually mean multiple opinions. Often, one or more "sides" evolve with differing approaches, motives, and perspectives on what kind of care and treatment is needed. Wayne had three siblings, an older sister, an older brother, and a younger brother. At seventy-four years old, their mother Beatrice was diagnosed with supranuclear palsy, a disease that involves atrophy of the frontal lobes of the brain. The symptoms are similar to Parkinson's disease, since the patient slowly loses the ability to walk and use the hands. Beatrice did not shake, as is typical with Parkinson's, but was wheelchair-bound and had not been able to easily use her hands for the last four years. Since the frontal lobes of the brain are involved, personality changes occur simultaneously.

For most of her adult life Wayne's mother was known for her remarkable disposition and ability to cope with a smile. But once her palsy became active, she became childlike and stubborn. The four siblings responded in different ways, eventually separating into two sides. One side focused on helping Beatrice accomplish what she wanted, and the other focused on getting their mother to do what they thought was best for the preservation of the estate, even if she didn't agree.

Prior to her palsy, Beatrice never showed anger, was secure and confident in herself, and was humble and unassuming. But in her illness, she became frustrated, insecure, frightened, demanding, and suspicious. She wanted her children to rally around her, spend time with her, and assure her of their support. Before her illness, she was ready to do anything to help them, but now she wanted assurance that they would do anything to help her. This type of "role reversal" in her relationship with her four children is not uncommon. She was no longer the serving parent. But she also wouldn't accept the four siblings as parent-like figures. Instead they were called to be her servants.

Wayne's older brother and older sister could not (or would not) accept the change. To them, Beatrice was no longer their mother. They foolishly bickered with her and tried to reason with her (but to do what they wanted, not what she wanted). Ultimately they fled from any responsibility for her. They were estranged from Beatrice in the last few years of her life, causing her to become bitter toward them. The disintegrating relationship was sad for her as well as for their entire extended family, and it also added to the difficulty of providing Beatrice with the care she needed.

**There is more at stake with estate
issues than the parents' belongings.
When strongly held differences become
argumentative and hostile,
the rest of the family can easily become
estranged. It's not worth it!**

When Wayne's father died at a young age, he left a sizable estate with Beatrice as the administrator. Initially, Wayne and his siblings helped their mother when she needed it. But major family struggles began ten years after Wayne's father's demise when the younger brother wanted to divide the remaining real estate in the family. The older brother and older sister wanted to continue to hold the land from the estate. Consequently, they made no effort to cooperate with Wayne and his younger brother, both of whom supported their mother's wishes, to settle the estate before her death. Wayne had assumed for years that when Beatrice was ready, the four siblings would all agree to divide the assets and close the estate. Unfortunately, he misjudged his sister and older brother's response. Over the next few years, they became more and more estranged from their mother as well as Wayne and his younger brother. By the time their mother moved to be close to Wayne so he could care for her, only Wayne, his younger brother, and their wives were willing to help her. The other two siblings would not help except on their terms. The result was infrequent visits by Wayne's older brother and no visits at all by his older sister after their mother moved.

This adversarial attitude was also an expensive one. When Beatrice could not get the older sister and brother to come and get things she wanted them to have from her house, she simply gave everything away to her friends. She sold her home to a neighbor well below market values because she wanted them to have it. This infuriated Wayne's older sister and brother and increased their hostility, deepening the rift.

**When siblings and parents
cannot agree on priorities
and objectives for potential
inheritances, everybody loses!
Remember: the parents have the final
say about their belongings!**

Wayne's sibling relations disintegrated. For over ten years, his older brother and sister barely spoke with him. His mother's health continued to decline until she needed major surgery. Wayne's wife became Beatrice's best friend, spending hours caring for her, helping her bathe, taking her to the grocery store, and taking her out to eat. Wayne's younger brother's wife also provided a lot of assistance. Wayne's children and his younger brother's children stayed close to their grandmother. But sadly, Beatrice did not see her grandchildren from Wayne's older sister again and seldom saw those of Wayne's older brother. One lesson learned from this experience is that a spouse can be a great help (or a major hindrance). Beatrice did not like or trust some of her children's spouses, but she deeply loved and trusted Wayne's wife.

When Wayne's mother died at the age of seventy-nine, she was bitter and lonely for her children and grandchildren. Wayne visited her three times a week. His wife, his younger brother's wife, and their children also visited often. They frequently brought Beatrice home with them, particularly during holiday occasions. Beatrice appointed Wayne as executor of her will and gave him power of attorney because she felt he was the only child who would not "fly into a rage" when she talked about their father's estate. After Beatrice's passing, Wayne and his older sister never spoke again. Fortunately, due to his wife's efforts, Wayne patched things up before his older brother's death. The seven-year period after Beatrice's health declined drastically was a sad and stressful time in Wayne's life, because he knew how unhappy his mother was, and there was nothing he could do about it.

Lessons Learned the Hard Way

After his long and stressful experience, Wayne made some broad observations relevant to caregiving:

* You never really know your siblings until you have cared for an aging parent and settled your parents' estate.
* If at all possible, try to accomplish the parents' desires regardless of whether it makes sense to you or not. It really is their estate. If they want to do something with their stuff and it is not harmful, help them do it. If you don't, they will usually find another way to do it anyway.
* Some siblings will not help solve a problem unless they can control the outcome.
* Many cannot cope with the parent-child role reversal that is often inevitable. Since this ultimately affects the outcome, try to identify this situation early and deal with it before it becomes a stumbling block.
* A spouse can be a great asset or a great liability. If the spouse is a liability, allow him or her to disengage rather than using manipulation to try to get help.
* There are worse things than "no help." If your siblings are unable or unwilling to help, do not try to force them. That will only make life miserable as they rebel and fight whatever you are trying to accomplish.

Much more is lost by disengagement than by remaining involved with your parent, even in a hard (and sometimes out-of-control) situation. Wayne observed that the burden of helping his mother was ultimately a great blessing. His faith deepened, and he learned a greater measure of personal strength and perseverance.

What to Do?

Once siblings recognize the needs emerging for their aging parents, these questions will come up:

* Which sibling should take the lead?
* How will decisions be made? What if not everyone agrees?
* How much should the children do? How much should the parents do?
* How are responsibilities distributed?
* How is accountability managed and assessed for each sibling's agreed-upon responsibilities? What happens if one or more siblings simply won't participate in the care of the parents?

These are tough questions, even if all the siblings get along well and work together productively. But often, parental caregiving can be an ugly time for siblings, culminating in nasty intra-family disagreements and even lawsuits. Having some of these discussions in advance can help ease the challenges. The August 2011 article "The 50-50 Rule" incorporates the findings of Dr. Ingrid Connidis and the work of Home Instead Senior Care Network to guide siblings through such common issues as gender expectations, distance and proximity issues, money concerns, inheritance and legacy matters, effective communication, and teamwork.[6]

Another great source for sibling collaboration in caring for aging parents is AARP's July 2013 online article, "Getting Along to Care for Mom" by Barry Jacobs, PsyD.[7] In this article, Dr. Jacobs gives helpful advice to adult children about moving past childhood sibling dynamics to collaborate in healthy ways. Here's a highlight from his article as he talks about the division of labor in caregiving:

---

6 www.caregiverstress.com/wp-content/uploads/2011/08/The-50-50-Rule-Helping-Siblings-Overcome-Conflict.pdf
7 www.aarp.org/home-family/caregiving/info-07-2013/family-siblings-aging-parents-jacobs.html

Few groups of siblings achieve a perfect division of caregiving duties: For reasons having to do with time, resources, proximity and personality, one or more almost always winds up taking more initiative than the others. This may, in fact, be a better way for the group to decide quickly and act fast. What's important is that every sibling be allowed to contribute in some way. Think about holding quarterly meetings to fine-tune the caregiving plan; this builds a more cohesive team and gives you a forum where you can acknowledge each sibling's contributions.

**Siblings working collaboratively
are a great blessing.
Siblings working at odds with one another
are a hindrance, if not a curse.
Set the framework for collaboration
early in the process.**

Siblings must be intentional and work together with their parents to develop a caregiving plan and to foster positive relationships. Despite any difficulties or personality conflicts, strive for early agreement on a process and a division of responsibilities. Above all, care and kindness should be practiced toward one another throughout this process.

Chapter 3

The Transition-Moving from Independence to Dependence

Aging in Place...Do We Really Have That Choice?

Why Do We Have to Change Anything?

Overwhelmingly, most of us want to live "at home" for as long as we possibly can. Furthermore, most people have not made plans for anything other than "aging in place." According to the AARP, 89 percent of Americans over the age of fifty want to "age in place." Even if assistance is needed in daily living, 82 percent still want to "age in place."

As adult children, most of us also don't consider other alternatives until one of our parents has physical or cognitive challenges that demand our help. Even if our parents are healthy and capable into their eighties or nineties, we usually assume that they always will live on their own. Realistically however, most adults of retirement age will need some type of care for an extended period of time. Hopefully, early realization of that will stimulate some early proactive assessments and preparation. That, in turn, will result in a better understanding and greater readiness to act when decisions about a loved one's future (as well as our own) are needed. Too often, when both parents are still "living independently" on their own, they walk a precarious tightrope of each compensating for the aging challenges of the other.

When one parent needs help, the other one often cannot continue to "age in place" alone.

The house of cards can easily come tumbling down. And when it does, it usually happens quickly! In how many senior households do both parents review and balance budgets? Or pay the bills? Or manage investments? In how many homes do both parents know what medicines to take and when? Or both manage schedules and appointments? Even if the more physical tasks of daily living (like housekeeping and yard care, for example) have been delegated to service providers, do both parents know who to contact for each of those services? In most cases, only one parent knows how to meet each of these needs.

The mind-set and actions needed to live independently are different than those needed to incorporate assistance from caregivers, no matter what level of care is involved. The family conflict and trauma often associated with life changes complicates things that much more.

**Both parents and caregivers
need to recognize when
"aging in place" is no longer viable and
address the transition to dependent living.**

A Long Road to Dependent Living

We've already discussed Harriet earlier in "Assessing the Alternatives." A divorced, single mother of two boys with only an elementary-school education but with an admirable work ethic, she retired at the mandatory age of seventy. Soon afterward, she was forced to quit driving a car when the state required her to get a driver's license—a ridiculous idea in her opinion, since she had driven a car her entire life without one. Although not being able to drive crimped her ability to get around, her daily walks kept her physically healthy. She was independent and frugal, living near the poverty level. Like most parents, Harriet was private about her personal affairs, never discussing her problems or her finances with either Seth or Don, her two adult sons. She got by on her small social-security and state employee pension checks.

The first indication of their mom's struggle to age in place came when a financial situation presented itself to her sons shortly prior to her retirement. She had to ask Seth, her oldest son, to assist her in completing her income-tax forms. For most of her life, she had filed her income taxes by herself. But now it was getting "more difficult," and she needed help. Although the two sons were surprised at her low level of income, they were also pleased with her ability to make do. She wanted to age in place and seemed capable of doing so. Since she took pride in her independence, her sons went along with her preferences. Several years after her retirement, she sold the house where her sons had grown up and, on her own (because she didn't want to be a burden), she moved a short distance back to her hometown to live near her older sister and brother-in-law.

For the next ten years, Harriet continued to age in place, not needing or wanting any assistance. Both sons lived a day's drive away from her (and from each other). However, they visited her regularly and took her home with them for several weeks during holidays and other occasions. During that period, Harriet had several eye surgeries, and both her brother-in-law and her sister passed away. Her nephew then moved into his parents' house next to Harriet and was able to provide consistent, objective, and independent feedback on her well-being, keeping Seth and Don informed and comfortable with the situation.

Shortly before her ninetieth birthday, Harriet fell and broke her hip. Later, she fell again while watching her backyard cherry tree being cut down. Finally she fell and broke her wrist while attempting to start her hand-cranked, gas-powered lawn mower. At that point, Harriet's sons' recognized that aging in place was no longer a viable option. After visiting with her, they retained an elder day-care service to provide female companions during the day, quickly followed by a heart-to-heart discussion. They told Harriet that the next time she injured herself, they would move her into an assisted-living facility near one of them. Her recurring cycle of injury, hospital stay, and rehab simply could not go on. Although she was not pleased with that decision, it prepared her for the day when she could no longer live independently. Reluctantly and subconsciously, she prepared herself for the inevitable loss of independence and the move. The final incident occurred a few years afterward, resulting in more than a week-long stay in the hospital with another month of rehabilitation.

Her sons decided to move Harriet into an affordable assisted-living facility near Don. On the day of her release, they brought her home, helped her pack, and moved her with very little resistance. Despite periodic complaints and her expressed dissatisfaction, Harriet was much more content than either of her sons had anticipated.

This seems to be a recurring pattern with many of our parents after the decision is made for them. Despite some expected grumbling (usually when the caregivers are present), once the parents' overall safety, care, and social interaction has been improved, the caregivers enjoy a greatly reduced level of concern, and the parent frequently also feels safer and less anxious.

**Despite their vocal dissatisfaction,
many parents feel
safer and more content than expected once the
decisions have been made that don't
allow them to "age in place" anymore.**

A Quick Trip to Dependent Living

"Aging in place" worked well for Jane's mom, Nell. She owned a home and a bit of property when her husband died at a relatively young age. After fifteen years, she remarried, and her new husband, Chris, moved in with her. For the next fifteen years, they lived in the comfort of this homestead with Nell's two sisters-in-law and Chris's family living nearby. Jane loved the idea of her mom "aging in place" under these circumstances. With Jane's children both married, she and her husband were empty nesters. Life was good!

When Nell's brother-in-law called to tell Jane that her mother had suffered a stroke, Jane was devastated. Nell had been the picture of senior health: a one-hundred-pound dynamo with hardly even a wrinkle on her face. Nell had become the caregiver for Chris as he increasingly manifested symptoms of Alzheimer's. She was tenacious and didn't hesitate to drive five hours to visit Jane several times a year. Of course, she struggled with some aches and pains, and her hearing wasn't what it used to be. But she was in better health than many people twenty years younger.

When Jane arrived at the hospital, she found tiny Nell swallowed up in a big hospital bed, but thankfully conscious and aware. Although Nell recognized Jane as her daughter, the signs of the stroke were obvious. The right side of her face was pulled down like putty. The vision in her right eye was affected and so was her speech. However, she could still see and talk. As she sat there for hours with her mother, Jane grew more and more anxious as she waited for answers. She soon discovered that the small rural hospital where Nell had been taken was short of doctors. In fact, it was so short-staffed that Nell's attending physician was a traveling doctor and had to work hard to spend time and speak with her before he left in the morning.

In the short-term, Nell could no longer live on her own. She would need to go to a rehabilitation center for extensive physical, cognitive, speech, and occupational therapy. Jane and her husband had to quickly confront the reality that Nell could no longer live on her own. As Jane faced immediate, critical decisions, she felt unprepared and unarmed. She found herself asking the following questions:

1. What constitutes a good rehabilitation center? What are the criteria that make one rehab center better than another?

Most importantly, what makes a particular rehab center the right choice for Nell?

2. Should she move Nell closer to herself (five hours away), or should she find a rehab center closer to Nell's home and her extended family?

3. Where could she go for information and help in making this decision?

Jane relied on the hospital staff's recommendation, which, thankfully, turned out to be excellent. Though the facility itself had seen better days (which is relatively common), its caring staff was trained in current best practices. The outlook for a successful recovery was extremely hopeful, and Nell received wonderful treatment and care. In fact, Nell was able to completely overcome the fallout of her first stroke. Within three weeks, she was back home, managing on her own once again.

Next Steps and Painful Discoveries

In the days after this incident, Jane discovered that Nell had been hiding things from her. Chris's Alzheimer's had progressed much further than Nell had led Jane to believe. Nell had sworn local family members to secrecy about his real condition in fear that Jane would want her to change her living arrangements.

**The desire to avoid dependent living
is strong in many aging adults.
But at some point living without
help is no longer an option.
We need to recognize when that
point has been reached.**

Jane learned from nearby aunts and uncles that Nell had become a round-the-clock caregiver for her Alzheimer's-inflicted husband. Because of the huge physical, emotional, and mental demands of caring for him, Nell was worn out and exhausted. Though Chris could still perform most of the activities of daily life, Nell had been prompting him, aiding him, or waiting on him as his mental faculties declined. But Chris's abilities had so greatly diminished that Jane placed him in an Alzheimer's facility within days of Nell's stroke. Of course, selecting the Alzheimer's facility was another big decision Jane was not prepared for. But in this case, she had few alternatives, so it was an easier choice, though equally stressful.

As mentioned earlier, Nell had achieved a nearly full recovery from the first stroke she suffered. But three weeks later, she suffered a second massive stroke and almost lost her life. She had returned home from the rehab center. Her daughter-in-law was in town and staying with her as they celebrated Chris's birthday with him at the assisted-living home. The next morning, Nell tried to get out of bed and make her way to the kitchen. But she collapsed and fell. Paramedics rushed her to the same hospital she had been in just weeks before.

This time her condition was much more serious. The new stroke had taken away her ability to speak and concentrate and also took much of her mobility and stability. Her right side was decimated. After a week in the hospital, Nell returned to the rehab center. But this visit would last one hundred days, until Medicare required that she be moved. During this time, Jane did some research and learned that one stroke often leads to additional, more severe strokes.

The trauma that Nell experienced devastated her body. It robbed her of capabilities that would never return. As Jane looked at her mother's drawn face and withered right side she felt sucker-punched. She was not prepared or equipped to provide the intense care Nell needed. She required therapy in cognition, speech, swallowing, stability, mobility, occupational, and basic life skills. Nell also needed constant supervision. She needed professional help from people who were not emotionally and physically exhausted from the demands of travel, career, and family in addition to caregiving.

Another unexpected reaction was the guilt. Jane experienced significant self-doubt (which is a common reaction) for not taking Nell into her home. Some of Jane's friends had been able to care for aging parents in their homes, setting an example. Although Jane felt forced to make a different choice for Nell's benefit, she often still wondered, "Am I just being selfish? Could I make it work to care for her in my home?" Jane had peers who thought she should be doing just that. She felt pressure from people whose underlying and unstated message seemed to be, "If you really loved your mother, you'd bring her home."

Fortunately, one experience helped solidify her decision and gave her peace. When she was visiting Nell in the rehab center, one of the therapists pulled Jane aside and said, "I recently went through a similar experience with my mother. If you're like me, you are struggling with guilt about having your mother here rather than with you at your home. What I learned is that I am my mother's daughter first. That is my most important role: to love and ensure my mother is getting the best treatment and care that she deserves. And sometimes that means it must be in a professional, clinical setting." This counsel resonated with Jane and her husband. Jane's role was to choose what was best for her mom. She was now convinced that she had made the right choice.

**Guilt and doubt are natural for concerned
caregivers making decisions
that impact their parents. But we
simply can't foresee all the
unexpected consequences. Get relevant
advice, avoid unnecessary stress
if possible, get enough rest, and then
make your decisions in love.**

Long-Term Care-Life after Rehab

With three weeks left in rehab under Medicare coverage, the staff came to Jane and said, "Nell's time here will soon end. The insurance will no longer pay for our services. Additionally, we believe that we have done all we can do for Nell's recovery. You can choose to have her stay here, but you will be paying us yourselves, or you will need to find her another place to live. We believe that with the progress she has made, she can manage her life in an assisted-living home." Since the cost of keeping Nell in the rehab center would be between five and ten thousand dollars a month (an unaffordable amount for Jane despite the fact that it was typical and reasonable), Jane and her husband had to explore other options.

Jane was glad to have the time to make an informed and workable decision. She deepened her pool of knowledge by talking with friends who had similar experiences with their parents. After examining multiple options, Jane decided to put Nell in an assisted-living facility in Nell's hometown so that her local family and church friends would have easy access to her. This decision put more stress on Jane and her family because of the additional travel required to visit Nell. However, Jane chose this alternative because she wanted to lessen the anxiety of change for Nell.

Nell made the transition into assisted living much more easily than anyone expected. She made friends quickly and seemed to enjoy her suitemate. The medical, administrative, and support staff grew to love her as one of their own family, even as she suffered subsequent strokes.

But Jane also discovered that visits from Nell's friends diminished after she was no longer a part of their weekly lives. So after a while, Jane began to explore another move to a facility closer to her own home, where she could be more active in Nell's life as her primary caregiver.

Other stressors for Jane included the care and maintenance of Nell's home, car, investments, insurance, and bills. Jane had to find someone to fix Nell's leaking roof. She had to find someone to maintain Nell's property. She had to establish a joint checking account with her mom, which was complicated by Nell's inability to speak or write and required power of attorney, which she had not established earlier. Jane also spent hours searching through Nell's house for her important papers, needed to care for her and her estate. More will be addressed on these subjects in later sections.

Many assumptions concerning our aging parents often change quickly. That doesn't mean the decisions were faulty. It simply means things change. When that happens, adapt and accommodate the "new normal."

Preparing for the Transition

As addressed earlier in this section, most people want to age in place as long as possible. That is totally understandable. Depending on the situation, it may even be a viable option for many people, but it will seldom last forever. Sooner or later, almost everyone must come to grips with the fact that one or both parents will need care and support outside their home and immediate family. It may be short-term physical support because of an accident or a stroke, or it may be emotional or cognitive support because of eroding mental or physical capabilities. This can include balancing budgets, making investments, or disposing of unnecessary furniture, household goods, or memorabilia.

**Although aging in place may be an option,
we are wise to consider it a temporary one.**

These needs can arise from either cognitive impairment (such as dementia) or physical limitations (for example, Parkinson's or stroke). But in any case, researching alternatives will pay large dividends.

The following sections of this chapter address the first major steps in a move to dependent living, providing a mini road-map for a variety of situations.

**A common thread in the vast
array of circumstances
encountered by all aging adults
is that everyone loses
their capabilities eventually.
Anticipate and prepare for it!**

It may be slow or fast. It may be through cognitive degeneration, physical degeneration, or a combination of both. It may occur in various sequences depending on health, genetic history, personal or institutional support, living environments, and a host of other factors. But most people will encounter a time when steps need to be taken to move beyond aging in place. It is substantially easier for us to adapt to evolving situations if we have anticipated change, even if we cannot predict the nature of the change.

Helping to Make Viable Choices

What's Next?

Making choices is one of the most difficult periods for both caregivers and parents after everyone has accepted the fact that "aging in place" is no longer viable or is not a long-term solution. Ideally, caregivers have already started the process incrementally by offering solutions for easier home maintenance, such as lawn care and housekeeping. Then more difficult choices are needed to simplify our parents' lives while still allowing them to age in place. Examples may include consolidation (or elimination) of bank accounts, investment accounts, property ownership, and the like.

Often, the most challenging decisions relate to living conditions. Should the parents remain in their home and obtain day-care assistance? Or should they get live-in help? Do they move in with their children? Or do they move into some form of a senior-living environment (whether assisted living or other alternatives)?

After the decisions have been made about the parents' day-to-day living arrangements (or, far too often, after that determination has been made for them by unexpected health conditions), many downsizing decisions are needed. Do they still need two sets of bedroom furniture, or is one enough? Do they still need living-room furniture to accommodate a dozen people? Do they still need that old stereo equipment, or will a decent, off-the-shelf sound system take up less space and provide adequate sound quality for their aging ears? What about the ping-pong or pool table? Elimination of any of these items enables comfortable living in smaller spaces, which will, in turn, require less maintenance and upkeep. But each item also has emotional attachments, so every one of these decisions is difficult. If a move is coming up, eliminating large items early and prior to the move will save on costs, as well as the follow-up heartbreak of disposing of the items after the move since there really wasn't room for them after all. Early decisions are better than later ones.

Nevertheless the hardest decisions are not usually about big furniture items. They are about the small things that take up less physical space, but provide poignant memories of past occasions, relationships, and other personal history. The hardest things to downsize fall into several categories:

* China, silverware, and displayed mementos
* Jewelry
* Photos
* Letters, diaries, certificates, and personal memorabilia
* Pictures, paintings, and wall displays
* Books
* Tools
* Sports equipment
* Holiday decorations (especially handmade ones from kids and grandkids)

Even a small box of these items can take days to sort through. Each item will usually be picked up and handled individually. Each one will bring back countless memories, making it difficult, if not impossible, to dispose of them. Though repetitive, the process of going through these memories is useful. Some items, say books, may be assessed, and then quickly disposed of as a gift to a charity. But many are saved because of a special memory or hopes of reexamining the item within a year or two, as we usually tell ourselves we'll do it when we have more time.

When those same items are revisited in a few years, it's amazing how often what was thought to be indispensable at the first review is found to be disposable the second, or maybe third, time. But if the first review had not been conducted, those items would still be retained. This is because we need time to let things go. When we initially examine these items, we recall the poignant memories. We tell ourselves that we will spend time looking at the items and organizing or displaying them, but not just now. When we see them again after a few years, we realize that we haven't done anything with them other than put them out of sight (and out of conscious mind). But we start to understand that the same thing will happen again if we simply put the items away again. Thus, things that were once indispensable become disposable in time—if not the second time we look at the items, then maybe the third or even the fourth. But in any case, the initial review and assessment starts this important process.

**Helping to negotiate the challenges
of downsizing can provide
significant support and assistance.
Doing so in a structured way
also helps us get more involved in their lives.**

Helping them make decisions about yard care or using a maid is a manageable way to let them know that you care about them. In addition, helping with the easy decisions usually isn't very intrusive and, as a result, is accepted more readily. Once you are involved with them in making these operational decisions, it becomes easier to get involved in the harder decisions about furniture or memorabilia.

The Memory Boxes

When Ken's wife, Nora, died, his daughter Ann helped him go through her things and sort items for saving, donating, and disposal. Her clothes were donated or thrown away with few thoughts and no regrets. Since there was no direction in her will, her jewelry was divided between Ann and her brother's wife. Ken retained all the dishes, paintings, china, and silverware since they were fully functional and still needed.

But Nora also had forty-five years of diaries, photos, and correspondence that provided a personalized version of history and her life since before the day that she married Ken. This included correspondence between Ken and Nora themselves, correspondence between Ken or Nora and their friends and relatives (mainly with parents, uncles, and aunts), correspondence between Nora and her children, limited correspondence between Nora and her grandkids, and children's drawings and artwork created by her kids and grandkids over several decades. Since the diaries and correspondence were too precious for Ken to dispose of and absolutely irreplaceable, they were packed and put in the closet to look at when Ken had time.

But Ken remarried within two years and quickly became preoccupied with other activities. That meant that the time he had planned to revisit these memory boxes never materialized. So the boxes sat in the closet, gathering dust. Within five years, since Ken's new wife naturally wanted to make their home her own (and not just memories of Nora), the furniture and most of the dishes and silverware were handed off to Ken's children. But he retained the boxes of memories, always intending to look at them again.

Twenty-one years after Nora's passing, Ken also passed away. His second wife gave the memory boxes to Ken's son, Claude, who, of course, promptly decided that these memories were too precious to throw away and put them in the closet to sort through when "he had time." Sounds familiar, doesn't it?

Within a few more years, Claude retired and relocated, so the boxes of Nora's memories were consolidated, eliminating many photos and letters because the individuals involved were not known to Claude, Ann, or other family members. At this writing (two years after Claude's retirement) those boxes have now been reduced to a single box. The remaining materials have been reviewed by Claude in detail. Claude has also taken them to his children and grandchildren for a family-history review, renewing many memories and reliving old times. But each generation knows fewer and fewer of the individuals involved. Therefore, each review eliminates a few more letters, photos, and diaries. If Claude had taken the time to review these with Ken, he could have identified the people in those old photos and recounted the events and circumstances. But since Ken and Claude always procrastinated until they "had time," those portions of family history are gone forever.

**Helping our parents to downsize
allows rich opportunities to relive
their histories. Don't be "too busy"
for those opportunities.
You won't regret it. Honor
them with an interest in
their lives: listen to their stories
and learn about their past.**

Moving Parents out of Their Home

After a long period of discussion about moving to an assisted-living facility, Dave's parents finally agreed. In hindsight, their hesitancy had been driven by trying to visualize how they could actually carry out the move. After it was over, Dave's dad admitted that he couldn't imagine how to actually do it since he was more of an idea guy than a doer.

Selling the house was not a big deal since Dave had their power of attorney and his wife was a realtor. But getting them ready to move took several steps.

*   Dave found a place for them to live about a mile from his house.
*   He organized an estate sale.
*   Dave and his siblings let their mom and dad pick out everything they wanted to take with them. This was a challenge since they moved from a four-bedroom house into a one-bedroom apartment.
*   His parents let the rest of the family pick out memorabilia to keep.
*   Lots of stuff was thrown out.
*   Many useful items were packed up to donate.

When they started, Dave's mom and dad both wanted to sort through their things. His dad gave up first. Every item he picked up reminded him of so many memories that he simply couldn't decide what to do with it. At best, he got through a few drawers in his desk.

Dave's mom wanted to keep everything. On her last trip through the house, she was in a wheelchair, picking up bags of stuff, and she didn't even know what was in them! When Dave eventually got her to stop, she still took more stuff than she could fit into her kitchen or the remainder of the apartment. Dave had to simply let her deal with that problem in her own way after they moved into their new home. Once they tried living in their new home (in assisted living) and it was too cluttered to live in, they decided on their own to get rid of more things until it became livable after several months.

> **We can facilitate, organize, and help
> execute, but we can't force our
> parents to downsize and restructure
> like we think they should.
> They need to retain a sense of
> control over their own lives.**

A few months after Dave moved his parents, his dad said he wished that Dave had convinced them to move a few years sooner to give them more time to go through their stuff and deal with their emotions. Most importantly, Dave's dad was happy in their new arrangement. The social aspects of the assisted-living facility lifted his spirits. He could always leave the apartment, take the elevator downstairs, and find someone to talk to.

The Credit Card

After Dave's dad died and his mom moved into another location in the assisted-living facility, Dave saw no harm in letting her keep her credit card. It would allow her some control in her life, and, besides, in an assisted-living facility, there weren't many options to use it—or so he thought. To his surprise, within a few months, his mom was spending money on inconsequential and often silly stuff. She bought a one-year subscription to a genealogy website, even though she didn't have access to a computer and didn't know how to use one. She bought every *Reader's Digest* book and series she was offered by mail. She subscribed to every magazine offer. Imagine accepting every mail order offer received, and you can visualize the situation! In six weeks, she spent more than $800 on mail-order promotions.

Dave had to take her credit card away, cancel subscriptions, and return things that had not been used. When he tried to reason with her and asked for the card, she complained that she needed it. Dave told her that if she didn't give it to him, he would cancel it, since he had her power of attorney. So she gave it to him but complained every week for several years. She even began calling him at home to beg for her card back. Sometimes she called so often that Dave's wife stopped answering the phone.

He tried giving her a small amount of cash (an allowance). Much to his surprise, this proved to be a workable solution. She now felt that she had some control and was able to buy things when she needed to. Since the opportunity to buy things didn't arise often in the assisted-living facility, she used the cash mainly when Dave or his wife took her out. But then she was under their supervision, so she didn't spend it on frivolous or inappropriate expenses.

**We can help our parents avoid
unnecessary expenses,
but we must use tact to be successful.**

Avoiding the Glut of Scammers

A great diversity of scams has become prevalent in the past decade, and all seniors are especially at risk. There are too many scams to attempt to catalogue or organize them into categories. Recent data indicates that for every 215 scam attempts, one person (usually an elderly one) takes the bait and sends money. A good scammer can get about 125 people to send money every week, usually netting from several hundred dollars up to several thousand dollars. The scams seem obvious to many people who are exposed to them regularly, but blackmail scams concerning grandkids, IRS tax scams, lottery scams, and others have proven to be effective.

Helping our parents avoid these situations is a worthy endeavor, but it also takes a bit of tact. We can't just say, "Mom, I'm concerned that you aren't savvy enough to avoid being taken to the cleaners by a scammer. You need my help." Yet all too often, that's exactly how we come across, even though we are well intentioned. A better approach might be to comment, "Wow! Did you see that scammers are succeeding in taking money from people in our area with the XYZ scam? It's pretty scary. Have you encountered anything suspicious?"

Once we are able to open a discussion about this subject without accusing our parents of being dense, our objective (for both our parents and ourselves) should be the following:

1. Offer to provide *information* to our parents *on the latest scams*, especially anything involving technology or the Internet, since they may be uncomfortable with these.
2. Offer to be a *sounding board* for any financial decisions, especially ones that come up quickly or need a fast response time.
3. Maintain up-to-date *information on resources and recourse methods* in case any type of financial exploitation is encountered.

In addition, gently probe your parents on a regular basis about suspicious telephone or online contact. Although the likelihood of a problem is still small, the impact of becoming a target is large, both financially and emotionally, once an aging parent has been victimized.

Reliving Memories. Planning for the Future.

The process of downsizing and making lifestyle choices is difficult. Helping your parents with this while they are still capable has many tangible benefits. First, it gets you actively involved in their lives when you can still make a significant difference. It also provides many opportunities for remembering events and occasions together. Surprising revelations often come out of these joint sessions that help each of you understand what the other was thinking at the time. If possible, do this with siblings too. These opportunities allow you to delve into your parents' lives and to understand their hopes, dreams, and disappointments. If you are interested in genealogies, you can find out about all those uncles and aunts you have. You can ask about people you don't know in the old photos. But it also gives you time to discuss what to do in the remaining years of your parents' lives, both to be helpful and to honor their wishes. We must recognize and embrace these opportunities whenever possible, and we will be helping to facilitate important decisions as they arise.

Setting Limits and Dealing with Guilt Trips

Guilt Happens

Most people who take any responsibility for the care of their aging parents will second- guess their decisions at some point. Seeds of doubt inevitably enter our minds and emotions, often producing inner turmoil and personal questioning. Some of those questions may include the following:

* Should we accommodate our parents (and disrupt our own lives) by moving them in with us?
* Can our parents continue to live in their own house by themselves? What if we provide daily care or round-the-clock care?
* How can we be sure they really need the professional care found in an assisted-living or nursing-home facility?
* Are we simply choosing the cheapest care rather than the alternative that is best for their long-term welfare?
* Have we conveniently chosen the solution (such as assisted living, nursing home, home health care, or companion) that enables us to live less encumbered by parental care?
* Are we shirking our responsibility or dishonoring our parents by limiting their choices or pushing our agenda?
* Are we sacrificing our own family's happiness to please our parents? Are we trying to accommodate each family unit that's involved?

When that inevitable guilt trip happens, our parents are unable to help us deal with it. They have enough to deal with themselves. So we must come to grips with our guilt by ourselves. It's useful to set limits—on ourselves and how we deal with the challenges, on our parents' activities, and on our interactions with others.

Our parents, whether on purpose or inadvertently, don't usually help assuage our doubts.

As we'll discuss in more depth later, not only are our parents losing many of their capabilities and possessions (which they worked hard to accumulate throughout their lives), but they are also losing their independence. So they are naturally upset. Even if they obviously need our help, requested our help, and were initially relieved to have us involved, they may sometimes engage in fantasy thinking, grossly overestimating their capabilities, and become nostalgic about how things used to be. Those times definitely feed their frustrations, but they can also trigger our doubts and inner turmoil. If parents are living in the caregiver's home, their protests and complaints can become a daily source of stress. If they are still aware of their surroundings while living in some type of dependent-care facility, their frustrations often become a major topic of discussion and dissent during our visits (if not the only topic). Too often, the intended "feel-good" visits with parents result in our own guilt trips.

Another phenomenon occurs when our own doubts are compounded by those expressed by others. If siblings are involved, those who are not the primary caregivers will often question every single decision. Even if they are actively involved in the caregiving, some decisions may produce unintended and unforeseen consequences. For every one of those decisions, at least one sibling will ask, "Did you consider...?" Too often, the decision will have to be revisited and explained again and again. No matter how well-intentioned those questions may be, they come across as unnecessary and unwanted nagging. This persistent questioning can fuel our original doubts and wear thin on our patience, ultimately stimulating short tempers and irritability.

In addition, caregiving, like parenting, seems to invite unsolicited opinions from all of our friends and acquaintances. They have their own perspectives and strong opinions (well-founded or not) on the best caregiving solutions and how to implement them. What a person views as "the best solution" typically aligns with what that person has done regarding his or her own parents' situation. But every situation is different, and one solution does not apply to all.

**To maintain our peace of mind,
we must learn to manage
our responses to others' opinions,
criticisms, and advice
from our parents and from others.**

As you start down the path of caregiving, understand that you will never achieve perfection, no matter how hard you try or how much you want it. Give yourself and others plenty of grace. Mistakes and errors in judgment will be made at some point, if not somewhat frequently. Bad decisions, disagreements, and even hurtful encounters can become opportunities to learn about yourself and the people with whom you are interacting. In offering others the benefit of the doubt and avoiding the arguments and contention that usually result from defensiveness, your much-needed energy and strength can be preserved for the tasks at hand.

Three Stages of Togetherness

After Paige's parents reached retirement age, they decided to relocate across several states to live near Paige and her family, including their only two grandchildren. Paige suggested they move into the same neighborhood, but Ted and his wife, Bev, decided on a less expensive house about twenty minutes away. This worked well for a couple of years, with Ted and Bev living their own lives and taking care of their own house and yard. They enjoyed meals with Paige's family regularly, attended church together, jointly celebrated family events (like birthdays and holidays), and even took weekend trips together. Their close proximity allowed the family to establish a closer bond than ever before. Paige's family was able to help Ted and Bev in little ways that were appreciated, and then reciprocated, while each family unit maintained its personal freedom and independence. The short distance from one home to the other established clear limits between them, while still being close enough to encourage regular interaction and support. Life was good.

Then Paige's husband got a job opportunity that he did not want to pass up, which often seems to happen after grandparents relocate to be closer to their children and grandchildren. But the opportunity was in another city about two hundred miles away. Balancing a career opportunity with the guilt of relocation was an agonizing decision. After some discussion, Paige and her parents decided they would consolidate and move into one house in their new location if they could find a place that met their needs. Fortunately, they found a larger house with a mother-in-law area that was readily converted into a second master bedroom.

After selling their house and most of their furniture, Ted and Bev moved in with Paige's family in the new location, beginning a period of living together that worked well for everyone. Ted enjoyed yard work and took care of the gardening, lawn care, and minor outdoor chores. Ted had been a carpenter earlier in life, and helped with many household chores and fix-it projects. Bev maintained their own bedroom area and also helped with household chores, including general cleaning and kitchen cleanup, which Paige hated. Paige cooked, and the two family units ate dinner together every night. Paige helped her parents with medicines, doctors' appointments, shopping, and in many other ways.

Paige was also happy to have her parents there for companionship and additional security when her husband was traveling. Ted and Bev still had their own car and helped with local transportation needs for Paige and her two kids when needed. Easily agreeing on shared responsibilities, everybody was generally satisfied and content with the joint living arrangements.

Nevertheless, minor issues popped up occasionally. When outdoor projects arose that required more muscle than Paige's dad could handle, Paige's husband and son periodically clashed with him. One hot summer day, Paige's husband and Ted were arguing outside about fence repairs, and both were losing their tempers. In her dry humor, Bev commented to Paige, "It looks like it's getting pretty hot out there!"

But overall, Paige's parents were cared for while they also contributed to the family's common good. An additional benefit was that many opportunities came up to discuss family history and gain new insight into Ted and Bev's lives.

**Life is never stationary for long.
It changes, creating
new situations for us to face, even
when things are working well.**

After about two years of this arrangement, Paige's husband Keith lost his job. They could no longer afford the large house. After a year of trying to establish his own business, Keith got another job, but this one was fifteen hundred miles across the country. The smaller rental house they all moved into was tight for the two families, even though Keith was not home much. He commuted for a year and a half to enable their daughter to finish high school before moving. Anticipating the move and not wanting to be a burden, Ted and Bev moved out of the joint arrangements, returned to their small hometown, and bought a modest home. When Keith and Paige's daughter graduated, the two of them relocated across the country and renewed long distance care of Paige's parents.

However, after a few years of living on their own again, Ted was no longer able to take care of Bev by himself, and they moved in with Paige once again. This time it was a permanent move, but somewhat easier than the prior situation since Paige's two children were living on their own.

Throughout all of these changes, living arrangements, and joint decisions, the family's bond deepened, despite the usual differences of opinion. Although Keith and Paige did not set out to deliberately create these circumstances, they were able to evolve with Paige's parents for the greater good of the entire group.

Collaborating on physical limits and a division of responsibilities helps establish an environment in which everyone's role is understood and acceptable.

Moving in with Mother-in-Law

Bill's parents, Lucy and Brad, had lived by themselves in the same house for more than forty years. Now in their late seventies, they were finding the stairs in their three-story house more challenging. They had to navigate two stories of outdoor stairs just to get to their car. As Bill himself was approaching retirement, he and his wife decided to build a home in which they could retire that would also accommodate his parents. Lucy and Brad agreed and even contributed some of the funds from their home sale to the construction of the new house for both families.

Since Bill was close to his parents, the solution seemed idyllic. It would enable him to take care of his parents' needs and maintain daily communication with them. (His mother insisted on daily phone contact anyway!) Plus Lucy and Brad were able to live on one level for almost all of their activities, eliminating their daily struggle with stairs.

Initially, this worked well. But Bill's wife, Lynn, and his mother both had strong personalities and their own ideas of what needed to be done and how—for cleaning, cooking, scheduling, and daily living in general. Before long, personality clashes occurred. Then guilt trips began. Was the care that Bill and Lynn provided worth these conflicts? Should they have searched harder for another solution?

Then, after a relatively short period of time, Brad became ill, needing hospitalization, followed by continuous home care. Lucy and Brad's bedroom was converted to accommodate a hospital bed. Both families added Brad's care to their list of daily activities. With Lucy now focused on taking care of Brad, the personality clashes lessened. New responsibilities and limits fell into place fluidly due to Brad's illness. But soon afterward, Brad passed away. A grieving Lucy had little to do, and the conflicts resumed. However, many of the limits established during Brad's illness remained in place, providing some needed structure that no one had thought to establish before moving in together. This structure provided a foundation for another decade of living together in relative peace, comfort, and security for all.

Reexamining Love and Limits

After Jane's mom, Nell, had a severe stroke, Medicare allowed a maximum hundred-day stay in a rehab/nursing home. When funding ran out for that stay, Jane moved her mom to an assisted-living facility that was two miles from Nell's own home. Jane was concerned that the new location might cause her some anxiety. However, it quickly became apparent that the traumatic effects of the stroke left Nell with no geographic awareness whatsoever. She didn't know if she was near her home or on a desert island. The stroke not only affected her spatial awareness, it took away much of her language and mental-processing abilities. Jane and her husband, Bruce, were often at a loss, wondering what Nell was thinking or, worse, if she was even thinking at all. Nell made sounds and used hand gestures, yet they seemed disconnected from reality.

But things changed. Two months into Nell's assisted-living stay, Jane and Bruce came for a regular visit. After acknowledging their arrival, Nell became animated and agitated. She made a noise that sounded like, "Stochkey," over and over again. In concert with this sound she moved her hands in the shape of a square. Jane and Bruce listened and watched her for several minutes, and Bruce interpreted her sounds and movements as meaninglessness. To him, this was the same type of communication he had witnessed from her over the past five months. But Jane, who had become understandably emotional in caring for her mom and had speech-pathology training, interpreted Nell's sounds and signs very differently. She turned to Bruce and said, "She wants me to take her to her house." Bruce was suspect of this interpretation. He was convinced that Nell's mental wiring was broken and that she was simply confused.

Jane remained convinced that Nell was asking to be taken to her house. This "demand" raised doubts in Jane about her decision to place her mother in assisted living. Nell could barely feed herself because of the muscle loss from her stroke. She had also lost the ability to communicate through meaningful speech or written language. Her equilibrium was impaired. Although she could walk, she shuffled everywhere she went, often using the handrails that lined the halls of the assisted-living facility. Though she was able to use the toilet and dress herself, she was bathed twice weekly by staff aides. She was also taking numerous medications that she could barely swallow and were beyond her ability to remember without staff assistance. Though Jane and Bruce were fairly certain that Nell couldn't live by herself at her home, seeds of doubt entered their minds and threw them into an emotional spiral.

Since they were visiting Nell in her assisted-living home at that time, Bruce jumped up to search for the resident nurse. He found her in her office and shared what had transpired. As Bruce blurted and blustered, the nurse listened with kindness and composure. When Bruce finally wound down, she spoke in a tone that assured him that she had heard these questions and addressed these fears many times before. She said this,

"I see Nell every day and have been paying close attention to her progress. Let me assure you that she needs to remain in this environment for her own protection. There is no possible way she can care for herself without professional assistance in an assisted-living setting. Though today's experience is new for you, Nell is acting in a very typical manner. Interactions with almost every one of our residents, when visited by their children, will make the kids feel guilty about having to keep their parents in assisted living. What Nell is doing is standard operating procedure for many of our residents. They believe they should be home. The worst thing that could happen to Nell would be for you to take her to see her house."

"After you and Jane leave, Nell will not speak to her roommate or any of our staff about wanting to go to her house. Only when she sees her daughter do thoughts of her house come to mind. Once you leave, those thoughts will leave her too."

Bruce wanted to hug the nurse. She confirmed their assessment, freed them from their guilt, and taught them a huge lesson. Love requires limits—not only in dealing with Nell in her diminished state, but also for themselves as caregivers. While they needed to regularly evaluate Nell's mental and physical process, Bruce and Jane also had to trust their decisions and follow through with them. They made a series of rational, informed, prayerful decisions that led to Nell being in this assisted-living facility. But the word *stochkey*, accompanied by a hand gesture, had caused them to question and nearly abandon those limits.

As a final thought, Jane and Bruce soon realized that the experts were right. Nell needed to be in an assisted-living setting. She continued to have strokes, although they weren't as severe. One caused her to lose consciousness. Her resulting fall left her with dozens of facial stitches. Without the immediate response of the resident medical staff, she would have been seriously injured. Jane and Bruce were simply not prepared to handle a situation like that. So Nell didn't return to either her own home or Jane's.

Jane and Bruce continued to seek out the counsel and advice of Nell's medical staff to see if her condition was improving and to understand what was best for her. They continued to set limits for Nell and themselves.

Thoughts on Limits for Living Arrangements

No matter what living situation will eventually result, some limits and boundaries will help maintain order and avoid confrontational situations to whatever degree is possible. In any situation, a working structure and mind-set are always important.

* **Establish workable and mutually agreed upon schedules:** for meals, doctors' appointments, shopping, and so on. If your

parents live separately from you, reminders may be needed. If they forget (and they will), be prepared to adapt and adjust. Anticipate these situations, and allow enough time so that you don't get stressed and upset when that happens.

* **Anticipate conflict:** Others—such as siblings, extended family members, and friends—won't understand your decisions and will often second-guess you at every step. When possible, avoid the subject with individuals like that. If that is not possible, prepare yourself mentally and emotionally for criticism. Then look for ways to end those conversations gracefully. Practice makes perfect! And you will have plenty of opportunities to practice.

* **Create forums for ongoing discussion:** When dealing with multiple siblings who share responsibility for your parents, plan regular times to discuss responsibilities and, if possible, rotate them among those willing and able to absorb them. This will enable others to understand the realities and different perspectives. Unfortunately, this arrangement among siblings is impossible or undesirable for some.

In situations when parents are living with you, to whatever degree it's possible:

* **Provide designated personal spaces:** Have distinct areas for them to decorate and maintain.

* **Share responsibilities:** Try to integrate everyone into regular activities with at least some shared responsibilities (such as meal preparation, setting the table, and cleaning up).

* **Plan regular times with your own family:** If necessary, find and use an elder companion-care service or day-care service to ensure that your parents are safe when you are not physically nearby.

If parents live apart from you, whether in some type of profession-ally managed facility or by themselves:

* **Visit often:** Visits are critical to assure them of your love, interest, and involvement. In our own experience, frequency of visits is often as important, if not more so, than the length of visits. Many short visits are better than a few longer ones.
* **Observe their care:** Make sure their daily lives and activities are in order, since these are often overlooked by the elderly and can be missed by even the best professional staffs due to less-than-desired patient-to-staff ratios. This includes eating, laundering, cleaning, and similar activities that most adults take for granted. If you still have children at home, involve them in assisting with these. It will build a bond with their grandparents that they will appreciate in hindsight, even if it's years or decades later. This also teaches children to honor and respect their elders, preparing them for taking care of you when the time comes.

Recognize that your decisions may lead to unanticipated situations with unexpected results. Expect the unexpected.

After gathering relevant information, simply make the best decision you can and monitor the results. Often, changes will be required. When that happens, adapt, and do it again. There is no reason to feel guilty unless you ignored your conscience the first time. If that happens, make the right decision the second time with a greater degree of confidence.

A Caregiver's Road Map to Dependent Living

Plans succeed through good counsel.
Don't go to war without wise advice.

—*Proverbs 20:18*

Got Plans?

When you have to make critical decisions about your parents' future medical and physical care, it can feel like you're under siege. Moving our parents from their home was one of the most daunting challenges we have faced. The traditional roles that evolve over a lifetime between our parents and ourselves can be reversed in the time span of one or two years—often, in much less time than that. That stressful process happens under enormous additional pressures as we balance our responsibilities and relationships with a spouse, children, siblings, our jobs, and other commitments.

The first step toward dependent living often begins a transition that continues for years or even decades.

Whether the initial change involves moving in with family or to assisted living or a nursing home, it often occurs in the midst of added stressors such as:

*   The death of one of the parents
*   A debilitating event, such as a stroke or a fall

* Planning for the end of life (i.e., developing a do-not-resuscitate order or housing plans for continued recovery or care)

If plans have not been discussed before the crisis at hand, then key decisions must be made with additional urgency and under even greater emotional and financial stress. Answers are needed that have never been discussed or even considered and, as a result, may not be readily available.

We had to make quick decisions for which we felt ill-equipped, alone, and unprepared—while also being in a state of physical and emotional exhaustion. We felt foolish for not having considered these decisions before circumstances forced them upon us. Fortunately, most hospital social workers are caring and knowledgeable about options available in every price range and for every circumstance. They can and will help. But they are not knowledgeable about our personal situations. If we have done no prior research, we must default to the limited recommendations of the hospital staff.

In reflecting on our own less-than-strategic, decision-making process, we've learned important lessons. Now, we see friends and relatives repeating our mistakes because no one wants to deal with these awkward situations. For these reasons, we decided to create something of a "road map."

Preparing for Life beyond Retirement

In a typical scenario, Joan and Gregg retired in their seventies. They lived ten more years in their home of thirty-five years, and then moved to central Florida to truly retire (still living independently, but downsizing significantly). It was just right for them with a small extra bedroom for visiting kids and grandkids. Their sons' families (including three grandchildren) lived a day's drive away but visited regularly, always looking forward to and enjoying the beach. Life was pretty good.

Since Gregg was older than Joan, they both expected that she would outlive him. After about five years, neither of them was able to drive anymore—Gregg due to dizziness and fainting and Joan due to respiratory problems. They got along by using taxis and calling on friends and neighbors for transportation. Before long, they needed help with daily activities and tasks too, so they sought in-home help enabled through a long-term-care insurance policy. To any independent observer, it was obvious that they were unable to live on their own. But even when family members and friends pointed this out to Joan and Gregg and their children, no one wanted to address the situation.

Then the unexpected happened. Joan passed away first, even though she was ten years younger than Gregg. Everyone expected that Joan would be the surviving spouse, not Gregg. The whole family, but especially Gregg, was shocked and unprepared for this.

During the six months prior to Joan's passing and the first few weeks afterward, Gregg's sons visited quite regularly, both with and without their own kids. But both sons had jobs and couldn't visit as much as desired. Gregg's friends and neighbors helped out quite a bit, taking him to run errands, go out to eat, and assist in other ways. In-home care continued during the daytime, but with new significance. Besides physical assistance, the caregiver also provided some companionship and was sometimes able to help Gregg with transportation. Nevertheless, Gregg was by himself most of the time. He was unfamiliar with Joan's bill-payment schedule, their investments, where their memorabilia was stored for safekeeping, and any of a host of other items needed for settling Joan's estate and moving on with daily activities. Furthermore, their children, both of whom lived a day's drive away, were also unprepared. They also expected Joan to be the survivor, and since she knew everything, they didn't feel that they had to know all the details. Now Gregg was unable to live independently but was reluctant, if not unwilling, to admit it. The children now recognized his inability to live alone, but they were not familiar with the range of alternatives.

This unfortunate situation illustrates the importance of meaningful two-way discussions and some type of a "road map" to guide the caregivers in circumstances like this. The parents and their two grown children anticipated and prepared for many situations with regard to selling their home, downsizing, and relocating. But none of them expected Joan and Gregg to become simultaneously incapacitated and unable to care for their own daily needs. Nor did they expect Gregg to outlive Joan. Even with regular visits by the children and in-home care provided on a daily basis, it simply wasn't enough. The hardest decisions had not been confronted yet and still had to be made.

Steps to Take

These circumstances are similar to countless others we know, including our own in times past. Sooner or later, more help is needed, but everyone is unprepared and sometimes even unwilling to step up the level of care. The best way to avoid this situation is to plan ahead and start the awkward discussions we all try to avoid. The rest of this section provides a short "road map" to help navigate through these challenging times. Like any road map used when traveling cross-country, this "road map" is not a detailed set of directions to get us to the desired destination. It merely establishes the likely path and anticipated circumstances along the way. One size definitely does not fit all. Rather it outlines a process to begin examining options, preferences, and alternatives. To be most useful, the process needs to be tailored to your own situation with help from those involved in the caregiving process—yourself, your family, your parents, and your siblings.

1. **Face facts**: Recognize and acknowledge the powerful pull of the "aging in place" phenomenon as early as possible. Don't erroneously conclude that since your parents are living at home and doing well that they will always remain "in place" until their death. The US Department of Health and Human Services website longtermcare.gov provides these sobering statistics:
   * Someone turning age sixty-five today has almost a 70 percent chance of needing some type of long-term care services and support in their remaining years.
   * On average, women need care longer (3.7 years) than men (2.2 years).
   * One-third of today's sixty-five-year-olds may never need long-term care support, but 20 percent will need it for longer than five years.

   The department's statistics show that one or both of your aging parents will need long-term care beyond what your family is able to provide by themselves.

2. **Gather information:** Become better-informed about your parents' current reality. Parents often do not see the long-range consequences of not sharing the truth about their

health and their situation with their adult children. So this will involve some independent research on your part to determine what their real status is. Find out and write down the names and contact information of their doctors, dentist, optometrist, CPA, financial advisor, insurance agent, and others as their situation warrants. If your parents are willing to help with this, that's a bonus. But even if they aren't, you will need the information sooner or later. Be vigilant and look for opportunities to obtain this information.

3. **Communicate:** Talk to your parents about their wishes for future housing prior to a crisis. Nine out of ten of our parents want to live at home for as long as possible, and many believe they will stay in their homes until they die. But statistics indicate that probably won't happen.

4. **Get the details:** Get informed as soon as possible about your parents' financial status. Start now. Find out where their important papers are located and start the process of getting access to them. This includes wills, powers of attorney (POAs), titles to property and cars, important loan documents (such as mortgages, car loans, and credit cards), investment accounts, bank accounts, social security documents, and insurance coverage. Sit down and speak with them about their social-security, investment, and retirement benefits. If you know nothing of your parents' finances prior to a stroke or other disabling medical condition, you won't find anything out once they can no longer talk, write, or communicate.

5. **Coordinate:** Talk to your siblings and others that may have an interest in them and be involved with their future care (for example, spouses from remarriage, which can be a great blessing, a huge hindrance, or anything in between). Though

none of us likes to discuss the fallout of aging on our parents, it's a subject that can't be avoided. Contact your siblings and set up a time to talk about how best to support your parents as they age.

6. **Initiate legal actions:** If one does not exist, establish an updated, valid power of attorney (which gives you the right to handle their finances) for your parents and a living will (which states their medical wishes while they are still living but not capable of making their own decisions).

7. **Research housing options:** Spend some time getting familiar with housing options for aging adults in the area where they will live. If your parents fit the norm, they will want to simply stay in place at home. But as stated above, the odds are that they will eventually need some form of long-term care either in their own home, at a long-term care facility, or both.

8. **Insure:** Talk to your parents early about long-term care insurance. In 2010, the average cost of long-term care in the United States was over $6,200 a month for a semiprivate room in a nursing home. A one-bedroom unit averages $3,293 a month. (US Department of Health and Human Services Website longtermcare.gov). That's unaffordable for many. Long-term care insurance can help alleviate these concerns,

9. **Get expert advice:** This chapter started with a quotation from Proverbs. Solomon, who wrote the book of Proverbs, is considered one of the wisest people to have ever lived. In spite of his great intellect and knowledge, he wrote several proverbs about the importance of getting good counsel and advice. (Check out Prov. 11:14, 12:15, 15:22, and 19:20.) As you attempt to figure out social-security, Medicare, Medicaid, life-insurance policies and premiums, and pension programs (not to mention choosing future residential-care settings),

you will feel like you're fighting one battle after another. And they're all interrelated. So the results of one decision frequently affect another. That really complicates things! Solomon's words will ring true, "Don't go to war without wise advice." Seek guidance and counsel from people who know best practices for dealing with aging parents. Numerous online sources can help. Universities in your area may have classes on gerontology that you can audit or take for credit. Visit a nursing home or an assisted-living home in your area to talk to the director. They will help you develop a frame of reference and a base of knowledge as you face future decisions regarding your parents' care. Aging in America has become too complicated to try to navigate on your own. We all need advice as we face this battle. The primary reason most of us don't do this is cost. But as we have pointed out repeatedly in this book, a few hundred dollars spent wisely and early can save many times that amount later on.

10. **Establish support:** Look into joining (or even starting) a support group. If you are a part of a local church, work environment, neighborhood, or another community of some kind, you have built-in resources that you probably never even think about. There are numerous people in your circle who are at different points in the caretaking process. Get together to share knowledge and support.

11. **Repeat:** Finally, intentionally develop a candid and open communication loop with extended family members who are in regular contact with your aging parents. This will go a long way toward guaranteeing an honest and accurate assessment of the current reality your aging parents face and the situations that you will soon encounter together.

Chapter 4

Dependent Living

Absorbing Their Household

Getting It All Together

Moving your parents into more of a dependent-living environment usually includes at least one short phase of working together to absorb their household belongings. Whether they enter a nursing-care or assisted-living facility, move in with you, or embark upon some other arrangement, the contents of their household must be absorbed into a significantly reduced amount of space. This difficult step of dividing their belongings among your home, other family members, a storage unit, or a new living space inevitably follows the painful downsizing process discussed previously.

If your parents move into a nursing home, there is typically no room for any of their own furniture. In that case, anything saved must fit into your home or a storage space. If they move into an assisted-living apartment, there is often no kitchen (which also means no space for china, silverware, and other pieces acquired over a lifetime). So again, all the kitchen furniture (as well as the dining room) and contents must be eliminated or stored somewhere. Space in assisted-living facilities is also limited for clothing and furniture (if any of their own furniture is permitted at all), so these must also be dealt with. If parents move in with you, your space must now accommodate one or two additional people and all of their belongings.

In our experience, no matter how much downsizing had occurred to this point, it was not nearly enough! You will likely have saved more items than can be absorbed. However, take heart. The obvious space constraints will quickly require your parents to approach downsizing with a new and focused attitude. Things that once seemed important and worth keeping at any cost often become disposable after a few months of cluttering up the home environment. When everyone has to navigate around the extra stuff on a daily basis, it soon becomes noticeable, and then often disposable. The situation frequently helps galvanize an important change in attitude.

When downsizing, consider shifting your focus: rather than choosing which items to eliminate, try choosing what to keep.

Living with what you really use brings joy. The rest is just stuff! It's painful at first, but when the space constraints become clear, you will be amazed by how many things lose meaning or relevance. This first becomes obvious to the caregiver. But in every situation we've seen, the parents realize it too. It might just take them an extra few months. It's wise to let them discover it on their own rather than to push them on it and create a point of dissension.

**As a caregiver, nagging your parents
about the need for downsizing
is not worth the resulting tension.**

Unless they are truly hoarders, the space constraints of their new environment will have the desired impact. If they really are hoarders, then nothing will work anyway. Tactful reminders can be appropriate, such as:

* "Wow, Dad! This place just didn't absorb everything that we thought it would. Have you got any ideas about how we can make it all fit?"
* "Hmmm. We expected to be cozy, but this feels a little cramped. We don't seem to have the room that we thought we did."

Helping them recognize the clutter or "coziness" can be an important step in eventually getting rid of it. But you can always soften things by saying, "I know we can work it out. There's no rush. Now that we have everything relocated, we can work on this at a slower pace." Just relieving the urgency is often a big relief. Also, framing it as a joint project by using the word *we* can let them know that they're not alone. On the contrary, when the situation is stated as, "You need to work it out," (rather than we) it comes across as accusatory, puts more pressure on them, and increases their anxiety, hindering progress overall. If you sense that they are not ready and don't want your help, then step back and give them the reprieve they need.

Now What?

Recognizing the need for more downsizing creates a new challenge— what do you do with the excess? Here are several options:

*   **Get professional help.** Professional "organizers" with a caring attitude can be located to help, but for a fee. This is a growing field, especially as baby boomers continue to retire. A local real-estate agent can often help with recommendations (since they regularly deal with the need to unclutter homes for resale).

*   **Hold an estate sale.** This is a viable approach when there simply isn't time or interest in going through a lifetime's worth of possessions. The sales agent will sell the house or everything in it that is not identified as a "keeper" by the owner. What isn't sold and still has value will be donated. And, of course, lots of stuff will be thrown away. The agent usually receives a percentage of the proceeds of the sale, so there is no money out of pocket needed.

*   **Get temporary storage.** The major downside of a storage unit is the monthly expense. However, it might be the right solution, especially if your parent is already suffering from the loss of a spouse or the emotional toll of the major transition. Temporary storage can be a viable step toward lessening their attachment to their possessions and the memories they represent. But be prepared. The stuff in storage is out of sight. That usually means it is out of mind too. Some stimulus will typically be needed to go through items in storage on a regular basis. If there is no stimulus, progress likely won't be made in downsizing. That means the stuff will still be there, and the fees must still be paid every month.

*   **Accept cramped conditions.** This option may be a harder reality for caregivers than their parents. However, if your parents' living conditions do not threaten their relationship, safety, or finances, and don't encroach on your personal living space, this may be the peaceful solution. Immediate and

ideal circumstances may be worth sacrificing to help preserve your parents' emotional health as well as your relationship.

Before addressing longer-term issues of downsizing and absorption of the parents' household, let's look at a few examples to understand the emotions and phenomena involved.

Phases of Donating and Downsizing

As Kyle and Betsy relocated to be close to their daughter and her family, they moved from a two-story house with a basement to a much smaller one-level house. They moved in two steps—first into a rental home, and then, about a year later, into their own home. Though they were excited about living in a one-level home again, they grossly underestimated the basement storage that their old house had provided. It was a huge storeroom.

During a nine-month process of downsizing prior to their first move, they donated many pieces of furniture and much of what was stored in the basement. They methodically eliminated items with emotional value and those they knew would not fit into their new environment. With sadness, they donated massive, antiquated stereo speakers that were among their first purchases nearly fifty years before. They also conveyed some furniture items with the sale of their house that uniquely fit their location, like a pool table and a kitchen breakfast-nook table and corner bench.

But less than a week after moving into their temporary rental home, they realized that there was no space for a half dozen large pieces of furniture that they had moved across the country. The furniture, which had great sentimental value just weeks before, was soon picked up by a charitable organization, and they let it go with relief, not remorse. When Kyle and Betsy moved into their permanent home a year later, they repeated this process once again. More furniture that had been "precious" was gone in no time when it didn't fit. The space limits forced them to give up things that they had emotionally wanted to save. And they gave it up gladly, thankful for the additional space that they needed and wanted.

Through many discussions with friends and family about the downsizing process, we find that this scenario is repeated time and again. Seniors who have suffered through downsizing often recognize, in hindsight, that they should have eliminated more stuff at the beginning of the process. They wanted to hang onto things that had great importance sometime in the past. Even though those extra things could not be absorbed into the new environment, they often rationalized:

"Maybe the kids will want it."
"Oh, we'll find a place for it—somewhere."
"We'll make it fit, even if it's a bit cozy." (read: cramped)

When you hear yourself making such comments, recognize that hard decisions are needed—and now!

Deciding what to keep is a better framework than deciding what to eliminate. This approach may save you the costs of multiple unnecessary moves and the resulting grief over the losses.

"It's Not My House"

When Beth's parents moved in, she and her husband had recently become empty nesters. For that reason, they were able to relinquish one bathroom and two bedrooms to accommodate her parents in their house—one room to be used as an actual bedroom and the other as a small den with a sofa, easy chair, and TV. To help make her parents comfortable, Beth initially arranged the furniture, but encouraged her parents to rearrange things to their satisfaction. She also didn't hang their pictures or display any memorabilia to allow them a greater sense of ownership as they made their own choices.

After a few weeks, Beth noticed that no changes had been made, and nothing had been hung up or put out on display. She offered some suggestions, which they accepted. But after more time, they still made no additional changes. When Beth discussed this with her mother she said, "It's not my house. I don't have the right to do anything different than what you want."

Even after several years of living together, Beth's parents never felt at home enough to decorate and arrange their own living spaces. Although it was frustrating for Beth, this behavior stemmed from her parents' desire not to be a burden and a degree of embarrassment at having to be dependent on their daughter. Beth learned to suggest alternatives to her parents. But when they didn't take any action, she simply did it for them. The few times it became obvious that they didn't like her choices, Beth made adjustments until her parents seemed more comfortable. That approach worked better for everybody than having to deal with the frustration from Beth's parents' discomfort in decorating her home, even though the spaces were theirs to do with as they chose. Beth honored their feelings while monitoring their preferences as well as she could.

The Electrician Wannabe and Other Hazards

Despite a reluctance to rearrange furniture or make living areas their own, Beth's mother, Alice, was fearless when it came to any interference with her TV time. Since Alice had Alzheimer's, she couldn't remember how to turn on the TV, which involved two devices—the cable remote and the TV remote. As long as her husband was there, everything was fine. But if he was unavailable, Alice had a habit of unplugging everything and moving furniture to get to the electrical connections. She often left their TV room in a shambles, with furniture pushed aside and light cords and TV connections all unplugged. Arranging the furniture in a way that inhibited her efforts didn't work; Alice just moved things out of her way.

In addition, since she had been an excellent seamstress throughout her life, Alice sometimes wanted to sew and make things. So she opened the sewing machine and tried to operate it. Fortunately, she was unable to do so, since it could have been dangerous for her. Beth finally had to move the sewing machine out of sight.

Alice created some challenging situations that required constant awareness to avoid unsafe situations. Beth's dad was helpful at times, but the responsibility ultimately fell to Beth to adjust their space to avoid the risks. Thankfully, this phase didn't last long before it passed.

Acknowledging the Sadness

The initial process of absorbing your parents' household is often fairly short, which is a blessing because of the emotional pain associated with that process. But downsizing will often continue as additional care and progressively smaller living arrangements become necessary. Each time is different, and each time is also still difficult. But it becomes somewhat easier over time. By far, the greatest challenge is the initial downsizing process.

**Caregivers should be sensitive
to the emotional trauma
faced by their parents as they
let go of their belongings
and shift their lifestyle to an increasing
dependence on others.**

Even though the parents usually enjoy being closer to family and spending more time with grandkids, they still face the sadness associated with losing their independence and giving up physical reminders of their past. Your sensitive recognition of that hard reality is much more helpful than making objective, detached observations. But you can remind them that they still have their memories and perhaps some memorabilia associated with them. Here are some examples:

"Mom, it must be really hard to let go of a lifetime of belongings. But the memories will always be there. What has downsizing felt like for you?"

"Dad, we appreciate all the memories that are represented here. Don't forget, many of them are our memories too, so we are also sad to let these physical reminders go. But we still have the memories. What are your best ones?"

This approach lets them know that you care, that you share some of their feelings, and that you want to listen to and understand their thoughts. Helping them express their feelings is important.

Be prepared—listening to your parents' memories takes time. But you'll be glad someday that you made them a priority.

Living Together: When the Caregiver Becomes "The Enemy"

Wow! I didn't expect that.

Once you've begun the caregiving process in any form, you'll probably view the loving sacrifices you make for your parents as altruistic and generous. Increasingly, you're taking on the stress of their living conditions (and maybe even home maintenance), their downsizing process, their financial security, their health challenges, and their life choices. You're facing difficult conversations about their well-being with your siblings or other family members. Perhaps you're also bearing the burden of new expenses related to their care.

So when your parents lash out at you because you're the nearest target for their frustration, it may feel like a shocking, thankless blow. At these times, it's helpful to remember what they're experiencing. Despite the fact that you have their best interests at heart, you are the most visible evidence of their loss of independence. Your parents are fighting a losing battle with their vision, their hearing, perhaps their mobility and overall health, their skills and occupations, and some of their cognitive abilities. If they have relocated, they also are letting go of their home, their friends, and their ease in transportation. Several of these losses often occur simultaneously over the same time period, compounding the effects and their impact. In these dark times, the caregiver may be viewed by the parents as their "jailer."

Intellectually, your parents might recognize that you really care for them and are their main supporter. But they may still blast away at you in their frustration simply because you are the most convenient and visible target. Like the valve on a pressure cooker, they allow the pent-up steam and frustration to escape. When this occurs, it often surprises and provokes the caregiver to lash back. Obviously, this response doesn't help the situation.

As a caregiver, being aware of your parents' challenges and frustrations will help you find ways to minimize the tension and avoid some unnecessary skirmishes.

Another aspect of this dilemma occurs when the caregiver's family gets involved. Perhaps your spouse says, "See? I told you it wouldn't work out. We need to do something else." Or the kids say, "When are Grandma and Grandpa going to get back to normal? I don't like them when they act this way." Now the caregiver is perceived as "the enemy" by both the parents and the rest of the household.

No matter how patient and caring you are, you'll probably find yourself reacting or retaliating, and then encountering a degree of depression at some point. There will be times when you may even want to retaliate by imposing some punishment. These responses will often be followed by guilt, whether due to an inappropriate response toward your parent or the seeming neglect of your own spouse or children. It takes a strong person to overcome these emotional reactions and guilt trips and focus on what you know is the right thing to do. Being aware of these natural reactions and anticipating them can be extremely helpful. Something as simple as having some prepared responses to fall back on can alleviate the tension while you regroup and pull yourself together again.

**Understanding what's happening
and knowing you're
not alone offers a measure of
relief. You're human and
need help coping with the stress
in these circumstances.**

Growing Pains

Ted and his wife had lived with their son-in-law Keith for about a year in two upstairs rooms, including a large bedroom and a den area. Ted spent most of his days watching sports on TV in the upstairs den. He had a hard time with the stairs, although he was able to negotiate them every day. He also still felt some responsibility for taking care of his wife, who had Alzheimer's. But Ted seemed to have no real purpose. As a result, he was depressed and often ornery. One day when he seemed unusually grumpy, Keith asked him, "What are you so mad about?" Since this was before Keith began to comprehend the losses Ted was dealing with, Keith said, "You have a pretty good life—no real responsibilities, no expenses except eating out and buying your own clothes, no cooking, no cleaning, and so on. You get to enjoy life by sleeping in, being entertained, enjoying nature, and having others take care of you. What else could you want?"

Ted wrinkled his nose, looked around at his surroundings, and grumbled, "I could use an elevator and a bigger room."

Keith exploded, "I'm not rebuilding my house or moving!" and stormed out of the room. Now both Ted and Keith were mad. Keith hadn't realized yet that Ted wasn't interested in a home renovation.

Ted always had been fiercely independent and a strong contributor in all aspects of his life. Now he was simply a bystander in his own life. And he hated it!

A Peace Offering

One day after the above incident, Keith's wife, Paige, decided to bake a coconut pie for Ted. No one else in the family was fond of coconut pie, so this gesture was specifically for him. After serving him a piece, he still sat grumpily, eating his pie and watching TV. So she asked, "How's the pie?"

He looked at it, scowled, and said, "I've had better!"

Needless to say, that was not the appreciative response Paige was expecting. So she took the rest of the pie (all but the one slice Ted was eating) while it was still warm and shoved it down the garbage disposal saying, "I don't want you to have to eat something that's not good."

He reacted immediately and said "Hey! It wasn't that bad!" That comment didn't help at all.

Paige left the room, fuming. Shortly afterward, as is frequently the case, she again felt guilt and remorse at her reaction. But her reaction was a typical human frailty. She was caught unaware when she did not anticipate Ted's grumpy response. This will happen to all of us more frequently than we'd like to acknowledge.

Hanging Around

After moving in with his son's family, Fred became depressed over the loss of control in his life. This was certainly an understandable reaction to the multitude of health issues and the undesired dependence on others. His despondency was obvious because of his sullenness as well as his posture. He often hung his head in a droopy position. His son tried fruitlessly to cheer him up with small talk about sports and news activities. One day when he saw this droopiness, he commented that Fred should try to avoid "that hangdog look" that was becoming commonplace.

Fred snapped back, "It's my head and I'll hang it wherever I want to!" Like many other little behavioral instances, his response caused a chuckle. But it also served as a reminder that the caregiver cannot control the emotions of others. Constant reminders, no matter how well-intentioned, may not help at all if they are not well-received. At that point, they turn into nagging and become a new source of irritation. That's exactly the opposite of what is desired.

> **When helpful intentions are not received favorably, avoid turning into a nag. Making it an issue will only worsen a precarious relationship.**

What to Do?

Negative responses are very human, even though they are not endearing. Most of our parents aren't looking for handouts. They didn't anticipate losing their capabilities and becoming more dependent on others with every passing year. They still want to contribute and feel that others will be interested in their contributions. They need a purpose. More will be said about finding a purpose in a later section. When they find and embrace a meaningful purpose, many of the conflicts can be addressed or accommodated more easily. There's less room for resentment. Then caregivers can focus on redirecting their energy toward helping parents focus on their new purpose. For now, we want to primarily recognize that these unpleasant reactions are natural, expected, and impossible to totally avoid.

However, it's important to grow more proficient in finding ways to de-escalate tensions instead of lashing back, calling names, or pointing out the shortcomings of those involved. We have been guilty of each of these responses at times, and strongly felt the resulting guilt. But just like Solomon recognized in Proverbs 15:1, we have also have seen how "a gentle answer turns away wrath but a harsh word stirs up anger." Practicing gentle responses under difficult circumstances can go a long way toward alleviating stressful situations.

A gentle answer turns away wrath. Really. Try it.

Changing Patterns of Life

Accommodating the New Normal

No matter what caregiving options are eventually chosen, both the caregiver and the parents will need to adapt and face significant changes in their patterns of daily life. This is one of the greatest trials. Caregiving activities become part of the new daily norm, requiring all those involved to adjust their family routines and traditions. Unfortunately, most of us embrace changes to daily patterns and treasured traditions slowly and reluctantly.

For many caregivers, significant time will be devoted to some form of medical assistance: managing daily prescriptions, scheduling visits to an array of doctors and dentists, dealing with unexpected emergency-room visits and short (hopefully) hospital stays, sorting through Medicare and Medicare supplement insurance, and accommodating other health-oriented activities. If the parents live with you, additional cleaning, feeding, and entertainment routines must be planned and accommodated. But even if they live elsewhere, caregivers will want to visit them regularly and take them for outings; shopping trips; and, of course, doctors' visits. Caregivers who had become empty nesters again have additional responsibilities besides their own care. Caregivers who are still raising their own children have substantially increased the number of people depending on them, compounding the complexities of daily living.

Caregiving responsibilities also become complicated when parents resist collaborating on decisions they're used to making independently. Many of our parents have prepared themselves for death—disposing of their assets, writing wills, taking care of funeral arrangements, and the like. But even in those cases, most people have assumed a quick death with no lingering impact. They have not prepared for a multiyear degradation of their capabilities and loss of independence that require someone else to take care of them. Naturally, they will resist this process. Very few of us expect or plan for the duration and difficulties of parents moving from independent living to a growing dependency on caregivers.

Caregivers and their families living at home seldom prepare to make these changes. Their inevitable sacrifices often include fewer vacations (if any), earlier mornings, and later nights just to accomplish their basic caregiving responsibilities. It often feels never-ending and can sometimes be overwhelming. But just like other aspects of normal living, it is a cycle.

Once you anticipate and accept the caregiving reality of regular life interruptions, you will adapt, and enjoy your parents more easily.

After every frustration and sacrifice, there is a period of satisfaction and reward. It may take time before that happens, but like the analogy used previously of raising kids, the satisfaction and fulfillment that come from taking care of parents is often delayed. After learning to expect that an array of frustrating, funny, poignant, memorable, and adorable situations will occur in unpredictable places and times, you will find it easier to endure and to adjust as needed. Simply put, that's life!

Time for Lunch

When Nancy's parents moved in with her, she took them to lunch at a nearby Bob Evans Restaurant during the busy days of the initial transition. That gave Nancy a break from preparing lunch herself and eliminated decisions about what to serve. However, this periodic lunch soon became part of the everyday routine. Nancy's mother, Betty, would come into the restaurant and declare, "Our kitchen's closed today!" Then she proceeded to order the exact same meal every day (grilled chicken, carrots, tossed salad, and apple dumplings). Within a few months, all the servers at Bob Evans knew exactly what she wanted every time she walked in the door. Betty felt comfortable and "at home" there. She started calling it Bob's, as if she were on a first-name basis with the founder.

But those were the positive aspects of this new pattern. There were also negatives. Obviously, the cost of eating lunch out every day for three people had not been anticipated or budgeted. But the most surprising aspect was that the lunch excursion to Bob Evans quickly evolved into a *required* midday activity—every single day. Furthermore, it seemed to be the highlight of Betty's day. As time went on, Betty (who had Alzheimer's) got ready to go to Bob's earlier and earlier. Sometimes right after eating breakfast, Betty came downstairs, dressed and with her purse in hand, saying, "I'm ready to go." When Nancy reminded her that she had just eaten, Betty insisted that she had not and that she was hungry and ready to go. Learning to handle this situation without an argument took skill and patience on Nancy's part. But it became a regular part of the daily routine for several years until Nancy's parents moved into an assisted-living facility.

As it turned out, the staff at Bob Evans were a joy that brightened everyone's day. The restaurant manager and several servers became like extended family members, with a mutual affection that lasted for years after Betty's final lunch there, and even beyond her passing. When Betty arrived each day, one of the servers asked, "Is your kitchen closed today?" Then everyone laughed. Once when Nancy apologized for Betty's inappropriate behavior, the server replied with grace and sincerity, "Oh, there's no need to apologize. We recognize their situation. They make our day! We enjoy seeing them and doing what we can to make them feel comfortable and at home." That gracious response comforted Nancy in the midst of the daily stresses she was experiencing.

At the end of the year, the restaurant even gave Nancy a holiday present, their own brand of sausage, for being one of the restaurant's best customers. Over time, Nancy noticed other customers who were there daily and saw that the restaurant staff treated them all like extended family. Many had challenging physical or emotional disabilities. The excellent and caring treatment by the restaurant staff, besides being a good business practice, brightened the day of these aging "regulars" at a time when too many people thought they were not worth the effort it took to deal with their additional needs. These small kindnesses were worth their weight in gold.

The Sheriff/Nagging Responsibilities

Darin's mom was healthy for most of her life, but she suffered from recurring back pains, which were initially triggered by a minor traffic accident in her thirties. When Darin became her caregiver, he also assumed the responsibility for her weekly physical therapy. As is the case for many of us (aging or not), when the pain got bad, she renewed her commitment to exercising, which usually helped a lot. But as her back improved, her commitment waned, and the pain returned. As physical therapy and home exercising became part of the caregiving routine, Darin became the alarm clock that reminded his mother about her physical-therapy appointments and home exercises. No matter how politely or tactfully he reminded her, his mother often saw Darin as a nag!

Over the years, his mom had back surgery several more times, but it never provided enduring relief. Her final surgery at age seventy-five left her bent over, which required her to use a cane for support. She also had an open wound that never fully healed, even eleven years following the surgery. Through many of those years, Darin continued to be "the nag" about his mother's therapy. Being viewed in this way does not make for an endearing relationship, even if everyone knows and agrees that the parent must be reminded to do the therapy or it simply won't be done. From the caregiver's perspective, it feels like we must be "the sheriff" that is enforcing "the sentence" to be carried out on the parent. That's no fun either.

Mixed Messages

Keith's mother-in-law, Alice, had Alzheimer's and lived with him and his wife. Keith asked his work associates not to leave work-related messages with Alice if she answered the phone at home. At this stage in her Alzheimer's, Alice could not remember to give a message to Keith, nor would she be able to write it down. When John, one of Keith's coworkers, called one day, Alice answered the phone. John introduced himself and said he had a complicated message to leave for Keith. He asked her to hang up and said he would call right back. He asked her not to pick up the phone, so he could leave a message on the voice mail. She agreed. In less than a minute, John called back. But Alice answered the phone again as soon as it rang since she was standing next to it and she had already forgotten John's request. Surprised, John patiently explained the situation again and asked her not to pick up when he called back. With her Alzheimer's, Alice could not remember to let the phone ring and let the answering system pick up. After four to five attempts, John finally gave up and called Keith back himself after a few hours.

It's important to remember that even when the challenges associated with handicaps like Alzheimer's are anticipated, we can never be sure exactly how it will play out. To maintain their sanity and composure, caregivers must be prepared to adapt to unanticipated situations and make friends and associates aware of the circumstances. In this specific situation, John and Keith had a good laugh whenever John recounted the story.

Companion Care-Paid in Full!

Soon after Beth's parents, Tim and Alice, had lived with her for a while, she became uncomfortable leaving them by themselves for any period of time because of their health problems. After some experimentation, Beth settled on companion care, an adult-sitting service, as a viable solution for those short times when she needed to leave them alone. However, they always insisted on paying the companions (although they also complained about the cost). Some of Beth's close friends were eager and willing to help when possible and without compensation. This was a favored solution since Tim and Alice knew these friends and enjoyed their company. But Tim and Alice also insisted on paying the friends, which created awkward moments, such as when Alice tried to force a twenty-dollar bill into the hand of one of Beth's friends after a visit. Several discussions between Beth and her mother changed nothing.

Finally, Beth started telling her mother that her friend had already been paid, and Alice certainly didn't want to overpay. Alice vigorously agreed! More surprising because of her Alzheimer's, this was something that Alice was always able to remember! Thus the solution of "she's already been paid" worked for several years.

Food for Thought

Rose's mother, Mary, enjoyed eating out, but she had Alzheimer's and had lost the ability to read. So when they went to a restaurant, Rose asked Mary what she was craving, and would then find an appropriate item on the menu. With her Alzheimer's, Mary's table manners had diminished a long time ago. So Rose asked for a table in an out-of-the-way spot in the restaurant, and then helped her as much as possible.

Mary often ate with her fingers. Once, Mary could not find her napkin, so she used the tablecloth (to the server's horror) to wipe her mouth. Alzheimer's patients usually revert to their childhood manners, which can be extremely uncomfortable for the caregivers and others accompanying them. But Rose and her family didn't let that deter them from the pleasure of eating out, and they almost always found others to be gracious and understanding.

Rose even carried some special business cards in her purse that read, "Please excuse my mother's behavior. She has Alzheimer's." If she noticed someone staring or if Mary's behavior was particularly childlike, Rose would hand out the card to other individuals as appropriate, without saying a word. Recipients would smile, find a graceful way to handle this situation, and obtain a small degree of insight into the challenges involved in caregiving.

In similar situations, Beth's mother Alice (who also had Alzheimer's) sometimes used maple syrup in her coffee, stirred her coffee with a knife or fork, and drank her coffee with a spoon in it (causing her husband to exclaim, "You'll put your eye out!"). Like a child, she stabbed her chicken breast with a fork, held it up like a lollipop, and took bites off it. She also ate thousand-island dressing on her ice cream and drank barbecue sauce with a straw, among other inappropriate behaviors. Each of these initially caused a degree of embarrassment for Beth and her family, and Beth often tried to stop or adjust the behavior. In hindsight, however, it seems that trying to change these behaviors was not worth the effort and conflict. Others really don't care and usually don't notice.

Hitting the Right Note

When Ralph's in-laws moved in with him, life changed in many ways. One was that he became the chauffer for many excursions. He loved to listen to country music when driving, especially if he was driving for any length of time. Early in their time living together, Ralph was driving his mother-in-law, Polly, while listening to a Willie Nelson album. He noticed in the rearview mirror that Polly was crying and using up her tissues as fast as she could pull them out of the box. Mystified, he pulled over to the side of the road and asked, "Polly, what's wrong? Why are you are crying so much?"

Her answer surprised him. She said, "It's so sad!"

He responded, "What is?"

She said, "What they're singing about."

Stunned, Ralph listened to the words of Willie Nelson's songs and realized they were all about cheating hearts, revenge, heartbreak, and a host of other marital, dating, and interpersonal life challenges. From that time on, Ralph was always aware of the radio music he played when chauffeuring his in-laws. Finding cheery, upbeat music to boost the mood was an ongoing challenge. The best answer for Polly was old-time gospel music, which she loved and always perked her up. The beat was usually strong enough to keep Ralph alert and awake behind the wheel.

Scooting Around

Soon after Ted moved in with his daughter Paige, they obtained a portable, battery-operated scooter for Ted to use to get around the mall and for activities that involved a lot of walking. A lifesaver for all, the scooter enabled Ted to participate in many activities that he otherwise would not be able to. It also made an outing easier for Paige and her family since Ted could keep up with their pace.

But the scooter also required a learning curve. The first time they took it to the mall, Paige's husband, Keith, dropped Paige, Ted, and the scooter off at the entrance to the parking garage while he parked the car. As Keith walked down the stairs from the upper-parking level, he noticed a significant traffic jam. Imagine his surprise when he discovered the cause of the bottleneck was Ted leisurely riding his scooter down the center of the street, holding up all traffic. Somehow he had gotten separated from Paige and couldn't navigate the curb in the scooter. Oops!

On a later visit to the mall, as Keith and Ted (on his scooter) were using the elevator to change to a different mall level, Keith held the elevator door open for Ted and several other mall patrons. He heard a distressed cry from inside the elevator and saw that Ted had pinned an elderly woman into the corner of the elevator and couldn't figure out how to get the scooter into reverse.

Keith and Paige soon learned that Ted needed to be accompanied to avoid any unanticipated issues with the scooter. Despite these periodic surprises, the scooter was a big help and enabled Ted to regain quite a bit of independence, helping his mobility while also improving his self-esteem.

Church Clothes

Going to church was important to Nancy's mother, Betty. Despite Betty's Alzheimer's, she enjoyed the singing and fellowship. But she enjoyed it so much that she dressed for it several days of every week. Often late on a weekday morning, when Nancy was least expecting it, Betty came downstairs into the kitchen wearing her Sunday best and declare, "I'm ready!"

When Nancy asked, "Ready for what, Mother?" Betty answered, "Why, ready to go to church, of course!"

Then Nancy had to convince Betty that it was not Sunday and she should change clothes. When Nancy was unable to do so, she let Betty wear her Sunday clothes for the rest of the day or until she decided to change herself. Keeping her clothes clean was not worth the frustration of trying to get Betty to change.

Similarly, in wintertime when the temperatures were well-below freezing, Nancy encountered a lot of resistance from Betty over wearing her winter coat. The answer was usually, "It's so nice. I don't want to get it dirty." Even when Nancy convinced her to take it along, Betty often left it in the car for the same reason. Nancy's rationale that "winter weather was what winter coats were for" never seemed to make any difference to Betty. As with many other off-beat behaviors, this was not worth an argument or disagreement, so Nancy often relented to Betty's demands rather than deal with the conflict. It was not worth the stress. Where to draw that line will vary from household to household, but the concept is one that will surely come up when living together or even when spending a lot of time with your parents. Choose what to disagree over carefully to preserve your sanity and your morale.

Midnight Surprise

One winter night, Rhonda and her husband, Tom, were awakened from a sound sleep in the middle of the night by the front doorbell ringing. Tom quickly threw on some clothes and answered the door. To his great surprise, Rhonda's live-in father, Jim, was standing at the front door in his pajamas in bare feet in the snow! Tom exclaimed, "Jim, come inside, before you freeze! What are you doing outside in the snow in the middle of the night?"

Jim replied, "I had to go to the bathroom."

To which Tom answered, "Why didn't you use the bathroom by your bedroom?"

Jim responded, "I heard the toilet running and didn't want it to overflow and make a mess."

Tom was stunned. Any counterpoint would have been useless at that hour of the night. No harm was done. No mess had been created. But this incident served to illustrate that good intentions of live-in parents can be dangerous no matter how innocuous the situation may seem. Jim could easily have gotten disoriented, lost, and injured in the subfreezing and snowy weather. Tom could not fault Jim for wanting to avoid a mess, although even if the toilet was running a bit, it wouldn't overflow from one-time use. No matter how diplomatic Tom could be, any discussion was bound to come across as a reprimand. Tom encouraged Jim to use another bathroom if that occasion occurred again. But Tom kept his fingers crossed that it wouldn't happen again.

That's Life!

When the caregiving process begins, most of us consider only the responsibilities, increased expenses, and reduced freedom in our lives. Those sacrifices are definitely there and have a substantial impact on our activities. Few caregivers anticipate the satisfaction and fulfillment associated with caregiving in advance. As already indicated, those rewards are often delayed, frequently by months or years. But once we commit to providing our parents with care and we have adapted to the changing patterns of life, it also becomes easy to find new joys and memories in the daily cycles of life. Recognizing and anticipating these changes and their unpredictable nature will help the transition and maintenance of the caregiving process. Looking for little humorous situations and victories in overcoming daily challenges helps us not only to maintain our sanity, but also to enjoy life's lessons. Life is a struggle. We might as well embrace it!

Navigating Medical Challenges: Doctors, Dentists, Medicare, Insurance, and Therapy

Worn-Out Bodies Need Attention

As our parents age, their bodies naturally become more frail, even if there are no other medical issues. But many aging seniors also suffer from specific ailments, pains, and disorders, which are often compounded by strokes or seizures. On the positive side, seniors often have more time during their retirement years to explore their health and medical options—and make these good habits part of their routines. Eating well and keeping physically active appear to significantly slow the aging process. Exercise is the primary mantra to staying young and feeling good. A study published in 1995 that tracked 9,777 men between twenty and eighty-two years found that physically unfit men who became fit had death rates 44 percent lower than those who remained unfit.[8] Furthermore, in 2010 those sixty-five and older spent about $18,424 per person on personal health care, "about three times more than the average working-age adult and about five times more than the average child," according to a 2014 study in the journal *Health Affairs*.[9] So this is definitely an area of importance to our parents and their peers.

Unfortunately despite those statistics, too many of our parents choose to live sedentary lifestyles, making their health situations worse. That's especially true for those in need of caregiving support. We can (and should) encourage them to heed all the available advice to get more exercise, eat healthier, and make other choices that are good for their well-being and health. But if they

---

8 www.medindia.net/health_statistics/health_facts/senior-health-facts.htm
9 http://content.healthaffairs.org/content/33/5/815.abstract

make bad choices, there isn't a lot we can do about it. We can try to remind them and to motivate them, but, in the long run, it is still their choice to decide how well to take care of themselves. It's not up to the caregiver. Nagging doesn't help. It will only alienate the parents and frustrate you. So when possible, choose to encourage in ways that will enhance your relationships and not put them in jeopardy. The relationships and memories, good or bad, will always outlast the physical bodies.

From a caregiver's perspective, we're often the ones helping them carry out their intentions with regard to their health and medical needs. No matter what living arrangement we have worked out with our parents, our daily schedules often fill up with some form of medical or health-related caregiving activities. In addition to helping them with scheduling appointments for doctors and dentists and physical therapy, you may be managing their daily medications, making unexpected visits to the emergency room, and staying with them in the hospital. You may also be driving them to a myriad of those appointments—perhaps even to the fitness center and the drugstore.

One major time commitment can be dealing with Medicare and supplemental insurance. Most of the medical costs are covered by insurance of some sort, but the coverage is often hard-won. The sheer volume of medical claims makes government and private insurance companies rich targets for fraud and scams. For that reason, there are many safeguards in place, resulting in a complex array of rules about coverage, deductibles, and copayments that make up a massive bureaucracy. This medical-care system was developed with good intentions, and it usually works amazingly well, but it can also be extremely frustrating.

To comprehend the problem, begin with the rules-based bureaucracy administered by civil servants who anticipate fraud. Then add the challenge of seniors living on tight budgets and their natural desire to find cost-effective solutions to protect them without bankrupting them. Now having all of this in mind, we can begin to understand the environment that caregivers confront when helping their parents deal with these issues.

But here's the good news.

**With few exceptions, we found
social workers administering
the health-care bureaucracy are
conscientious counselors
who really care about helping people.**

The first crucial step is to contact the appropriate agencies and discuss your situation with them. Here are a few recommendations for this process:

* **Prepare to wait**. As frustrating as it is, be prepared to wait whenever you need to contact a health administrator. This is true whether it's on the phone or in person. Give yourself plenty of time, and don't exacerbate the situation by waiting until the last minute or trying to accomplish something on a short and demanding schedule.
* **Make personal contact**. If possible, visit the agency or organization in person. That allows some kind of "connection" to be made with the responsible individual. It also prevents the possibility of being disconnected on the phone and having to start over on a call.

*   **Make friends, not enemies.** Those helping you are trying to do just that—help you and your parents. They are not your enemy. So don't treat them that way. Friendly interchanges will produce much-better results than hostile ones.

Here to Help

Paige's parents had spent all of their assets and were destitute. In case you haven't dealt with Medicaid yet, that is a requirement for eligibility. After conducting some preliminary research, Paige decided that it was time for them to apply for Medicaid assistance, so she visited the local state agency. She spent the morning filling out paperwork and waiting her turn for an interview with a social worker. Although the interview was cordial, Paige was surprised by some of the questions but answered them to the best of her ability. Eventually the social worker put down the papers, looked at Paige, and asked, "Why don't you just tell me what your situation is and what you are trying to do."

So Paige explained:

*   Her mother had Alzheimer's, and her father had congestive heart failure.
*   Her parents had sold their house and had exhausted the proceeds supporting themselves.
*   Her parents had lived in her home for several years before moving into an assisted-living facility.
*   Her parents' assets were running out, and Paige could not afford to underwrite her parents for very long.
*   She needed Medicaid assistance.

After a few more questions, the social worker agreed to file for the appropriate Medicaid support. When Paige asked the social worker what she was trying to determine with her questions, she was surprised by her answer. "State and federal lawmakers have good intentions for Medicaid legislation. They want to help people, avoid fraud, and maintain an affordable program. But when they decide on new laws and regulations, they don't research existing laws very well. The result is a complex mishmash of laws that often contradict each other and differ from state to state. Fraud and abuse reduces available assets even more, so I'm responsible for assessing applicants' needs and motives. If I believe the needs are justified, I point them to regulations that will help applicants make their case. But if I think they are trying to misuse the laws or they're not in genuine need, I can just as easily point them to regulations that will deny their applications."

Although the ambiguity of this approach was shocking to Paige, a little research quickly confirmed the truth of the social worker's comment. Many regulations directly oppose one another. As the state legislatures and executing agencies try to straighten out the discrepancies, laws get passed that create new ones. So it is a never-ending challenge!

**Strive to achieve friendly interchanges
with social workers,
even in frustrating circumstances. If
you are assigned a social worker
you don't get along with, consider
requesting another one.**

The Training Alternative

Although most of our parents know that they should exercise to feel better and to be healthier, it is tough to do it alone. Judy, like many of her peers, really wanted to develop a routine for weight training and regular aerobic exercises. However, she lacked the discipline to follow through on her desires. Her husband kidded her saying, "A good streak of any of those exercises is one time in a row!" He offered to exercise with her, but it seldom seemed to work out for both of them at the same time.

The breakthrough happened when Judy decided to use a personal trainer at her community fitness center. The regular weekly exercise made a lot of difference in how she felt. It was an investment that was well worthwhile, even if it was only once a week. In time, Judy also started midweek routines, and her husband went with her.

It's difficult to change any routine, but sustaining a regular exercise routine seems to be especially challenging. The good news is that the effects are quickly noticeable, providing lots of incentive to keep going. You can help look for others to accompany the parents or to find tricks or incentives that will get things started. It is definitely easier with encouragement and support from others!

I'm OK? Not really.

Tom had a variety of physical ailments that needed attention and for which he routinely took prescribed medicines. He often did not feel very well. To the surprise of his daughter, after Tom had his checkups, he said the doctor didn't recommend any changes. On a subsequent doctor's visit, she decided to go with him. When the doctor asked, "How do you feel?" Tom's answer was, "Fine!"

So she chimed in with, "Daddy, what about...?" and triggered a realistic discussion of his ailments. This was probably the first time he had mentioned many of these. Despite the litany he recited at home, when he was with the doctor, he didn't want to describe them.

Sometimes our parents are reluctant to be truthful with medical practitioners because they fear a potential diagnosis or treatment, especially if it requires a change in their habits or requires them to refrain from things they want to do. This is all too common with our parents' generation. They don't want to complain, and they don't want to be forced to take corrective actions. So they cover up their aches and pains at the worst time—when it can make a difference. Though we can't force them, we can encourage them to be transparent with their physicians if they want to get better and reduce their pain.

A Happy Tune

Nancy's mother, Betty, was in her mid seventies before her family recognized her advanced case of Alzheimer's. Although she didn't recognize people and couldn't take care of herself, she was usually happy. Betty had a beautiful voice and loved to sing, especially old-time gospel songs.

When Betty went to the hospital for short periods, Nancy's greatest challenge was making sure she stayed in her room and didn't wander. But she was usually good-natured and often sing-ing. One of her favorite songs was "When the Roll is Called up Yonder, I'll Be There." She sang it regularly. Each time, after she fin-ished the song, she smiled and said, "I really will be there!" Despite her Alzheimer's, Betty always encouraged her family with her great attitude.

One day when Nancy arrived at the hospital, she noticed a tech-nician walking down the hall on her mother's floor humming that song. Later she heard a nurse softly singing the same song—half a floor away from her mother's room! Betty's love of God and her life-time of singing had given her everything she needed to bless oth-ers, even in the midst of a mentally debilitating disease. Nancy also was encouraged to see her mother's contentment and the power of her lifelong habits, despite her Alzheimer's. The caregiver often carries the greatest burden of this disease while patients have little, if any, stress.

**Despite long hours and many ongoing
frustrations of caregiving,
there are rewarding moments
with your parents bringing
poignant relief and real satisfaction
at unexpected times.**

In contrast to her mother, Nancy's father Ted had congestive heart failure and made regular visits to the hospital. Unless drugged up with painkillers, he maintained a full cognitive awareness of his circumstances. Ted was mainly limited by his physical challenges. When he was in the hospital and his family physician asked how he was feeling, he said, "I feel like I'm in jail!" While that brought a chuckle to the physician, it also made his caregivers aware that he needed encouragement and cheering up.

Your parents' differences in circumstances and attitudes should be considered when dealing with their needs. Ted needed encouragement while Betty often lifted up all those around her.

Midnight Disturbance

Both of Paige's parents were in their late seventies when they moved into her home. Paige's father Ted was on a prescribed blood thinner, making even minor scrapes potentially hazardous. One night, Paige and her husband woke up to the sound of panicked yelling and screaming. Paige ran to her parents' bedroom and saw blood everywhere—on the bed; all over Ted's pajamas, hands, and face; and even on the bathroom walls.

After examining Ted and helping him calm down, Paige's husband, Keith, said, "It looks like a nosebleed to me. Can you jam a handkerchief into your nostril to stop the bleeding?"

Ted replied, "No, because then I can't breathe!"

In the meantime, Paige had called 911. Within minutes, six burly firefighters were upstairs, assessing the situation for themselves. The senior EMT among them said, "It looks like a nosebleed to me. Let's jam a tissue into your nostril to stop the bleeding!"

Ted again replied, "No, because then I can't breathe!"

The EMT was more confident in his diagnosis than Keith had been, so he insisted, "Sure you can. Breathe through your mouth." Then he promptly plugged the bleeding nostril and began some minor cleanup of the blood. Ted was taken to the emergency room for further examination, but, fortunately, that was the full extent of his injury.

This incident illustrates several facts to consider as a caregiver. First, even minor issues can be frightening. Being awakened in the middle of the night creates panic and confusion for all—and is often not conducive to rational and calm responses. With the tension amplified by the bleeding, even a minor nosebleed caused a major panic. Second, although a nosebleed is not usually a big problem, when compounded by Ted's blood thinner, it quickly turned into a threatening issue. Although Keith had the right instincts, he was unsure of his diagnosis, so he didn't insist on a response like the EMT did. It helps if caregivers have enough knowledge and confidence to deal quickly and rationally with situations that occur. Finally, even a minor incident like this can require a major cleanup.

Medical emergencies cannot be predicted.
The whole family must be flexible,
adaptable, and responsive.

This event was no one's "fault," so it was inappropriate to try to blame anyone. It was an unfortunate lesson learned. The mess was just a part of life. Ted already felt badly about the results, so blaming him would have jeopardized fragile relationships. This wasn't the first unexpected cleanup necessary, and it wasn't the last. Better to just count blessings that nothing serious was wrong rather than initiate a fruitless finger-pointing exercise.

The Lost Specimen

When Rhonda took her father, Jim, for a checkup, he needed to provide a urine specimen but was unable to do so. As a result, the doctor allowed Rhonda to take a specimen jar home to return the following day with the desired urine specimen. Once Rhonda and her dad arrived home, he sat down in the kitchen to watch TV. He set the specimen jar on the kitchen table to remind himself that it was needed before he went to bed that night.

A few hours later, Rhonda returned to the kitchen. Her dad was still sitting in the same seat, but the specimen jar was gone! Upon closer examination, she noticed the top of the specimen jar on the kitchen table, but not the jar itself. When questioned, Jim could not remember if he had been able to provide the specimen or where he might have left it—most likely unsealed! Had it spilled? Was there an undiscovered mess somewhere? Everyone was in a panic to find that jar. All were greatly relieved when Jim soon found it—in his pants, of all places. Rhonda never knew whether Jim had tried (and failed) to provide a specimen in the kitchen or not. Certainly stranger things had happened. This incident reminded all that leaving him alone and unmonitored for long could have severe housekeeping consequences.

Winning Despite the Losing Battle

Despite the best intentions of the caregivers, parents, and health-care professionals, it is helpful to remember that we are still fighting a losing battle. Death and loss are inevitable. But quality of life and its duration can definitely be enhanced by cooperative and informed care as well as affordable insurance coverage. Don't avoid medications simply because of their expense (if they are affordable at all). The savings is not worthwhile if your parents are in constant pain. Conversely, they may also be so drugged up that they are completely unaware of their surroundings and companions. Neither of these alternatives makes much sense. Finding the balance between these extremes is a constant struggle. Recognize that we are conducting only a holding action with the possible gain being a few more years with an improved quality of life.

With that in mind, take the opportunity to set limited goals associated with medical care and therapy. Then celebrate them when they are accomplished. Set personal goals to use periods of necessary togetherness to improve your relationships and learn more about your parents. Then celebrate them when they are accomplished. Finding small joys in the losing battle of health care will make the process easier and will enrich your relationships. If you can also find ways to include your children, your parents' friends, and even others, the spark in your parents' eyes will convince you that it was all worthwhile.

Maintaining Connections

Easing the Transition

As you assist with new living arrangements for your aging parents, it is important and extremely reassuring to help them maintain connections with their friends, family members, and personal history. These connections soften the traumatic transition to dependent living and provide comfort and familiarity in the midst of all those changes. Family and friends also directly support your efforts as a caregiver by the help they give you and your parents. Here are a few ways to be intentional about encouraging your parents' connections:

*   Help maintain contact with long-time friends.
*   Celebrate occasions like holidays and birthdays.
*   Make every effort to attend one-time events like weddings and funerals.

Prioritizing Your Parents' Friendships

Maintaining friendships is an obvious and important key to helping your parents adjust to changing circumstances. But it doesn't "just happen." It takes work, planning, and thoughtfulness. You might consider retaining a close proximity to family and friends as you make decisions about new living arrangements, though that option often isn't possible.

When parents relocate, even if it's in the same general area, they are often unable to maintain easy contact with friends. Especially if those involved can no longer drive, it's up to the caregiver to arrange visits and make time for them. However, these circumstances also can serve as painful reminders to our parents of their loss of independence. Even with a caregiver willing to arrange the transportation, our parents will often downplay the importance of this contact (not wanting to be a burden) and allow themselves to become isolated.

If friends are no longer in close proximity, those relations may stagnate and atrophy a lot faster than expected. In these situations, you can seek out ways to encourage your parents to make new friends. But no matter how well-intentioned, making new friends always takes time and is often unpredictable and unmanageable. We can do everything possible to arrange the right environment at appropriate frequencies, but it's still a hit-or-miss situation.

**Helping your parents stay connected
with friends and family will ease
their transition to dependent living.
But it takes time and forethought.**

Other means of staying in contact with friends and family members can play an important role, whether by phone, letters, e-mail, or Facebook or other social media. But once again, although the caregivers might think the costs are minimal, the parents (usually coming from a mind-set of frugality) may not want to impose or be a financial burden. In that case, providing "prepaid" capabilities may be the easiest way to assure them that their socializing is encouraged and prioritized. Even if that capability is a natural and integral part of a cable of satellite Internet/TV/phone package, just explaining that it is prepaid may make them more comfortable.

Making the Most of Family Occasions

Recurring family occasions also play important roles in the continued well-being of our parents. When you include them in joyful events, you remind them of other good memories and also create new ones. You'll have the opportunity to draw them out with questions about past events and give them the chance to share their stories. Even if they deflect your questions at first, when you seek out their memories, you make them feel valued and appreciated. You also gain insight into their lives and history that you might not have otherwise known. It's so easy to overlook these opportunities to engage our parents and learn about their heritage. You have to be intentional. Here are some questions to help get these conversations started:

* What was the best birthday (or holiday) that you remember from your childhood?
* How did you grow up celebrating Christmas? Did you do anything differently than we do now?
* Did your family have Easter egg hunts when you were growing up? What were they like?
* What other unique holidays or special events did your family celebrate? How?
* Can you recall a Thanksgiving when you felt particularly thankful for something? What were the circumstances?
* How were your family traditions different as children? How did you reconcile and maintain these after you married? Did you create new traditions for our family that were not handed down from either of your parents?

No matter what occasion is being celebrated, open-ended questions like these usually lead to fun discussions for everyone, from youngest to oldest, while honoring your parents in memorable and enjoyable ways.

**Family celebrations create wonderful
opportunities to make
new memories with your parents and
show interest in their past experiences.**

Participating in Milestone Events

Weddings, funerals, and family reunions provide similar opportunities for memories and discussions but include a broader range of family members, friends, and even past acquaintances. These interactions often provide a treasure trove of memories and insights if we take the time to go—and then listen. While the primary focus should remain on the honorees, we can still acknowledge our parents' roles in how the entire family arrived at this unique event. With discretion and care not to reopen any unexpected old wounds, questions like the following can be valuable windows into our family history:

* Mom and Dad, did your parents approve of your wedding to each other? Or were there concerns? How were they resolved?
* Did we have any family members who were really different? Anyone that went against the grain? How did the family accommodate them?
* How well did your family cultures mesh? How did you work out any differences?
* Was your family part of a broader community (like your church, neighborhood, or ethnic groups) with similar backgrounds, interests, and traditions?

* How have you maintained both of your "roots" in family traditions?

These and other questions provide prime opportunities to explore the ways our families have evolved. As you help your parents maintain friendships, participate in recurring family occasions, and attend important family events, you provide rich opportunities to draw out your parents and share their lives and experiences.

Making Time for Friendship

Bill's mom, Lucy, lived in the same house near a downtown area for almost fifty years. She worked in a bank close to home, so she never learned to drive. When necessary, her husband drove, or she could take the bus. She was able to walk almost everywhere else—to work, the grocery store, church, and many other essential places. This kept her healthy, and it was convenient. Her closest friend for most of those five decades also lived within easy walking distance.

When Bill retired, he and his wife built a house with an in-laws' area for his parents. However, shortly after they moved, Lucy's husband became ill. He could no longer drive her to her usual places, or even to visit her longtime friend. Taking the bus became too challenging for her because of the longer, more complicated routes. So Bill and his wife decided they would offer to drive Lucy to see her friend or pick her up so Lucy could visit with her at their house. Although Lucy was not able to see her friend as frequently as before, she continued visiting this way for nearly twenty years until she passed away.

The lifelong continuity of this friendship sustained her through new surroundings, her husband's severe illness and passing, and her eventual move into assisted living and then a nursing home. Visits with her friend during those years gave Lucy something to look forward to every week as well as a treasured confidante. For Bill and his wife, these visits were worth the travel time and inconvenience because they always lifted Lucy's spirits. Their decision made a positive impact on the daily well-being of everyone involved (not to mention Lucy's friend).

When Things Change

Jane's mother, Nell, lived about an eight-hour drive from Jane. That wasn't a concern since both of them drove the distance regularly and easily in a single day. Nell was healthy and a go-getter. However, when Nell's health was compromised by a series of strokes, she had to be moved to an assisted-living facility. After much consideration, Jane and her husband decided to keep Nell close to her own home so that her friends could easily visit her. Despite the inconvenience to Jane, she wanted to provide the best possible conditions for Nell's full recovery that could be encouraged by her close friends. Unfortunately, that never happened.

As the situation evolved, Jane discovered that Nell's friends were not as mobile as Nell had been. Nell had been the most outgoing and active of all her friends. So after she moved, her friends visited her only a few times because they were unable to navigate the trip on their own or find someone to take them. Jane and her family visited when they could. But because of the distance, those visits didn't occur often. The nursing staff at the assisted-living facility cared for Nell and paid attention when they could. But they didn't have time to dedicate extra attention to those who needed it, like Nell. So she was essentially left alone, disconnected and isolated from anyone she loved.

In hindsight, it might have been better to locate Nell closer to Jane's home where she would be visited regularly by her own family. These lessons are often learned the hard way, by trial and error. It's important to reassess an evolving situation and make necessary changes if circumstances do not turn out as we'd hoped. But this is a difficult thing to do.

Despite your best intentions, decisions won't always result in the outcome that you intended. That's no reason to feel bad about your decisions. Chalk them up as lessons learned (there will be many) and move on.

Finding New Joy in Birthdays

Even though Bev had Alzheimer's, she always enjoyed birthdays and special occasions. She loved receiving presents and being the center of her family's attention. Her daughter Paige celebrated Bev's birthday with a small cake and other goodies, which always brightened Bev's countenance. Receiving a gift delighted Bev—just from holding the present, all wrapped up with bright paper and ribbon. However, Bev didn't understand that she was supposed to unwrap the present. She just enjoyed the attention of those she loved.

Paige encouraged Bev, saying, "Mother, let's unwrap it, and see what it is." But once the present was opened, Bev was no more joyful than she had been with the unopened present. She didn't understand the uses of the gift, whether it was clothing or photos or any other item. So there was no need to labor over what to buy her or what color to get.

In time, Bev's family learned that only one present was needed at these occasions. If there were too many, visitors sometimes worried that Bev wouldn't get around to opening them. When Bev sensed their anxiety, her mood quickly dampened. Focusing on her and showering her with attention and love was the greatest present she could receive.

At a birthday celebration, Bev always asked, "Have we sung 'Happy Birthday' yet?" No matter how many times the group sang the birthday song, Bev asked about it, again and again. And every time it was sung, she smiled and basked in the attention. The love and attention Paige and her family provided Bev were the best gifts of all.

**The best gifts for your aging
parents are your time and
your love. Don't worry about giving them lots
of "stuff" that isn't appreciated nearly as much.**

Making the Effort and Keeping Your Sense of Humor

Beth and her husband decided to take her parents with them to their daughter's wedding, knowing it would be a daunting task.

They flew across the country via commercial airlines despite the challenges of Beth's mother, Alice, having Alzheimer's and her dad, Tim, being very frail.

For several days, the four of them stayed with lifelong friends, the Joneses. Since the Joneses had helped care for Alice on previous occasions, they knew how to prepare their home and stay flexible under the circumstances. Tim enjoyed the opportunity to have easy conversation with friends who were interested in him. Since it was a joyful occasion, Alice was also happy and in excellent spirits. However, she kept forgetting that she was the guest. She regularly told the Joneses to make themselves at home and help themselves to food in the kitchen. When she assessed the guest bedroom where she was staying, she declared that she'd wanted to change the curtains and tried several times to take them down. Though Tim was embarrassed, everyone reassured him and played along, allowing Alice to play the part of a gracious and entertaining hostess.

At the rehearsal dinner, the wedding reception, and other festivities, both Tim and Alice greatly enjoyed visiting with friends and acquaintances. Tim enjoyed recounting his memories in his many conversations with friends and family. Despite the extra planning and effort to include our aging and frail parents in these events, the payoff can be worthwhile. Just remember to stay flexible, keep your sense of humor, and find joy and comfort in making this tangible effort to honor your aging parents.

Maintaining Connections: Hugs and Laughter

The natural process of aging often results in an unexpected degree of isolation:

* Retirement reduces or eliminates job-related connections.
* Illness or injury interferes with regular contact with friends and family. (Even if visits occur, the quality of interaction is often not the same.)
* Death of peers, especially a spouse, permanently terminates important connections.
* Communication difficulties, especially in hearing and in vision, create a feeling of being left out of conversations.
* Losing the ability to drive reduces independence.

Since quality interactions with those we love have a huge impact on our well-being, when several changes occur simultaneously, a significant degree of loneliness can result. Even worse, that unintended isolation can feel like a punishment (similar to sending children to their room when they disobey). The results of isolation quickly become obvious: increased pessimism, lack of interest in personal care and appearance, a loss of purpose, and clinging to others when it is time to separate.

We have to be sensitive and deliberate to help our parents face circumstances like these. When life gets busy, it's easy to forget or abandon our best intentions. More frequent contact with friends and family members, even if in shorter durations, creates a greater sense of inclusion. Besides actual physical contact, we can make phone calls, write e-mails, or use social media (depending on the comfort level of the individuals with these technologies). All of these can be helpful. If you can't find the right solution, keep at it. Look for areas of common interest with your parents that will help you maintain contact with them yourself.

Providing them with needed transportation has lots of additional benefits. Car trips enable your parents to get out more, give you more opportunities to connect with them, and often accomplish errands and appointments—all at the same time. As you check things off your list, you can chat with your parents, give them hugs, and laugh together. That extra contact will make a huge difference in their attitudes. Eating together, encouraging their hobbies, or learning something new together provide opportunities for quality interactions. Remember that hugs and laughter are great tension relievers. These genuine efforts strengthen relationships and give joy to all. In times of conflict, genuine caring and affection can help reduce stress levels.

**Include your parents in activities
of daily living to keep them
connected and feeling valued,
minimizing any potential isolation.**

As a final thought about meaningful connections, a great solution can be pet ownership. Pets can stimulate feelings of great joy and appreciation. If pet ownership is not possible, many organizations provide senior-friendly pets (usually dogs) whose sole purpose is to provide some level of love and companionship to aging people, even if only on a short-term basis. Those are all worthwhile.

So make extra efforts to include your parents in your daily life activities and communication, and use those opportunities to show love and concern.

The Emotional Roller Coaster of Aging

The Wild Ride to Dependent Living

As our parents first encounter the transition from independent living to dependent living, we often think of it as a one-time event. Then we'll be done, and everything will return to "normal." But that's not how it plays out at all. Rather, it's a slow transition with many ups and downs and a continuing series of highs and lows for everybody involved. Most of our parents are fiercely independent, do not like handouts, and want to earn their own way. So they are reluctant to admit that they need help, especially from their kids. They are the parents! They're used to being the helpers to their children, not the other way around. They certainly don't want to be a burden to anyone. When they finally acknowledge that they really do need help, their adult children should listen up and respond immediately.

> **Asking for help is a huge emotional
> downer for the parents.
> By the time they ask, their
> circumstances are probably
> more extreme than you think.**

Most of our parents encounter a dichotomy of thoughts about retirement. On one hand, they anticipate retirement as no work and all play—hobbies, sports, entertainment, travel. Freedom! But on the other hand, our parents have a growing awareness of their limitations and eroding capabilities far greater than their children perceive. Yes, many of them may be living "the good life," but they often conceal an increasing dread of dire circumstances hitting them when they least expect it: receiving scary results from medical tests, absorbing an unforeseen and unrecoverable financial setback, suffering an injury during routine home maintenance, and being victimized by a scam artist. We often don't detect (or take seriously) our parents' anxieties—perhaps because we're buying into the retirement dream ourselves.

When one of our parents' secret fears becomes a reality, the realization for the children is often abrupt—a wake-up call that we're not expecting. We recognize, perhaps for the first time, that our parents may have grave limitations, and our own future role may look more like a busy caregiver than a happy-go-lucky empty nester. Hence, the roller-coaster ride begins. But two distinct aspects of this ride are integrally intertwined: that of the parents and that of the caregiver. The rest of this section addresses the parents' roller-coaster ride and hopefully provides some help for the caregiver. In the next chapter, we'll discuss the caregiver's own wild ride.

We've already shared many ups and downs of aging in previous anecdotes and vignettes. But here's a snapshot of typical emotions that many of our aging parents will experience over time:

* **Low:** The despondence and embarrassment that comes from realizing that help is needed and dependence on others may become necessary.
* **High:** The relief of discovering that someone in your family understands, cares, and is willing to help.
* **Low:** The depression and emptiness experienced in disposing of lifelong possessions.
* **High:** The freedom that comes from having fewer responsibilities and possessions to manage.

* **Low:** The frustration of slowly surrendering vestiges of independence like driving, money management, and home maintenance, among other things.
* **High:** The satisfaction of watching kids and grandkids grow up and taking advantage of opportunities to influence their development (especially knowing that grandchildren are the parents' responsibility—not their own).
* **Low:** The periodic anger at themselves and at others from the major conflicts and minor disagreements bound to come up when living in close proximity to loved ones.
* **High:** The comfort of knowing close friends and relatives care deeply and are willing to listen.

It really is an emotional roller coaster! But too many people, both aging parents and their caregivers, don't understand that. Often, we want to live a devil-may-care existence and ignore the onslaught of challenges. Or perhaps, we choose the other extreme—focusing only on the grief, the annoyances, and the unexpected setbacks. Joy in the aging and caregiving process comes in facing the challenges with both honesty and hope.

Despite the loss of capabilities, delights and jubilation can be encountered just around the next corner. The parents are dealing with the onslaught of emotions surrounding these changes. Though dealing with your own emotions as the caregiver, you can also provide your parents with helpful support and perspective. When things are on a downtrend, try to remind them of the good times and provide encouragement and hope for the next upswing. When you reach the peak of a joyful solution or memorable event, don't just jump on the euphoria train. Rather, steady yourself and your parents for the next downswing with an honest outlook.

Some families experience years between each successive high and low, while others may go through several phases in a short span of time—like weeks or months. We never know how long any phase will last, so both parents and caregivers should enjoy the positive ones as much as possible. In a relevant biblical example (1 Kings 18:16–19:19), after Elijah the prophet soundly defeated the four hundred prophets of Baal on Mount Carmel, his nemesis, Queen Jezebel pursued him across the land. Immediately after Elijah's big victory, he was running for his life and soon became despondent. When God came to Elijah as a gentle whisper, he allowed Elijah to express his negative emotions; assured him of his allies; gave him an action plan, and provided him with a companion and confidant, Elisha. Caregivers can follow this example.

When our parents hit at a low point, we can definitely help! Allow them to express their negative feelings. Then collaborate with them on an action plan. Reassure them of support. Offer companionship.

In the face of painful or inconvenient circumstances, we can take time to reflect on past blessings and anticipate joyful surprises that may be in store. In an earlier chapter, when we discussed downsizing, we recommended that the focus be on what to keep rather than what to let go. A similar focus is helpful throughout the emotional roller coaster for the aging. Focus on what can be done with the capabilities that remain rather than despairing over those that have been lost. That just may be the action plan needed.

Don't misunderstand—this is hard! Remember, aging is not for sissies. But it takes balance. If we ignore reality and take too much of a "Pollyanna" outlook, we won't be ready for impending crises common to aging people. But if we despair, we won't be able to notice and enjoy the blessings. The caregiver can help provide this balance, without being a nag or a wet blanket. Be the companion and confidant who will encourage your parents when needed.

Lightening the Load

Kevin was down in the dumps over his rotator-cuff surgery. Even after faithfully doing his physical therapy for a year, he had regained about 80 percent of his pre-surgery capability. Despite this limitation, he continued to participate in some sports activities he enjoyed, especially tennis. One day when his shoulder was bothering him, he complained about it.

Another player Jim, who was about a decade older than Kevin, listened to Kevin's complaints and commented, "Yeah, that was a bad one."

Kevin replied, "What do you mean?"

Jim said, "I've had both knees replaced, both hips replaced, and rotator-cuff surgery on both shoulders. The rotator-cuff surgery on my dominant side was by far the worst one. It took several years to regain the capabilities I have now. But what are you going to do? Do as much as you can with what you have, or sit around and feel sorry for yourself?"

Jim's response shocked Kevin. Feeling embarrassed and guilty, he resolved to stop complaining and develop a different attitude. He adopted Jim's mind-set as much as possible. Shortly afterward, Jim faced another setback when he fractured his ankle. But true to form, he had the surgery and recovered once more—a little weaker physically but with the same spirit of making the best of it. People like Jim inspire us and ease the responsibilities of their caregivers substantially. But even if our parents don't adopt a positive mind-set, we can choose to follow Jim's example and lighten the load for ourselves and for everyone around us.

Tossed Away?

Tom's attitude was the extreme opposite of Jim's in the previous vignette. He often felt inferior to others and believed that people were taking advantage of him. As a younger man, he was an excellent carpenter and a good problem solver. But he never felt good about himself and regularly felt victimized. After his retirement, he and his wife moved close to their only daughter and their grandkids. They bought a small house and worked in the garden, even winning "yard of the month" in their new location. With the yard as a major focus, life was pretty good.

But once Tom lost the ability to work outside, he never developed other interests. He primarily watched major-league baseball and game shows on daytime TV. Inactive and unfulfilled, his health slowly declined. He constantly felt sorry for himself, so his emotional health also atrophied. After several years, when Tom went to the hospital at various times for care, he often complained that he had nothing to live for. He'd say, "Just toss me in the back of the pickup truck, and throw me in the river." This also depressed his daughter and the rest of the family, but no matter what they said to him, he was frequently very down.

This lasted for several months before he finally passed away. Sometimes, caregivers can encourage other interests in their parents to help stave off depression in times of physical infirmity. But if your parents are facing clinical depression, you won't be able to talk them out of it. If they won't seek help from a doctor or psychologist, then you should consider getting professional advice yourself on how to help them.

Aging and Addiction

Bob had always been a go-getter and enjoyed increasing levels of success for most of his career. As a college athlete and an entrepreneur, he faced plenty of setbacks too. But he always bounced back. Bob was in his late sixties when he started having problems with his health. He experienced fainting spells, extreme fatigue, and loss of mobility. His doctor advised a series of tests, but they revealed no major concerns. One night, soon after a significant financial setback, Bob took to his bed. He could hardly move and was soon nauseous and shaking violently. Over the course of the weekend, Bob suddenly realized what was happening to him—he was detoxing from alcohol.

Bob had always been a social drinker, but in the midst of life stresses, perhaps exacerbated by aging, he had developed a debilitating habit of alcohol abuse. During a visit for the holidays, soon after his illuminating weekend, Bob admitted to his daughter Lynn and her husband, Keith, that he was an alcoholic. Though Lynn and Keith had detected Bob's dependency on alcohol for many years, they had never seen him in a state that they would have described as drunkenness. Bob had always taken good care of himself, shown a positive attitude in the ups and downs, and maintained tremendous physical strength for his age. But in eighteen months, Lynn and Keith had observed Bob's rapid decline in health, which was particularly obvious since he lived in a different state and they saw him only two or three times a year.

Despite Lynn and her family's pleas to get help, Bob refused to enter rehabilitation or active recovery. He felt desperate to recover his financial losses from earlier that year and did not want to take the time to focus on his health.

Lynn knew nothing about addiction, so she surrounded herself with experts and researched treatment options for her dad. She visited more regularly, but she also followed the advice of those counseling her in the habits of an addict, which often meant painful encounters with her dad. Caregivers should be aware that addiction can become more pronounced and destructive late in life. Though Lynn's father drank alcohol regularly his whole life, it had never grievously affected him until he was a sixty-eight-year-old man. If you suspect your parents are dealing with addiction, it's important to seek out support. A good place to start is a local Al-Anon Family Group—the Alcoholics Anonymous counterpart for an addict's loved ones. Experts suggest you attend at least six Al-Anon meetings, trying different groups, until you decide if it's right for you.

For Lynn, trusted friends from her church, including one who had dealt with an addicted child, were most supportive at the height of her dad's crisis. After her dad finally entered recovery, Al-Anon helped Lynn deal with the emotional aftermath.

Alternatives to Aging? Not really!

If we, or our parents, become fixated on what has been lost, we will always be in a state of mourning. Capabilities and circumstances will continually decline, and injury, addiction, or illness will only compound the situation. But there's no alternative to aging. Although some of our parents may get to the point of wishing for the end, we must try to stay focused on our blessings, even when we are tired and worn out.

**If your parents persist in depressive
attitudes or destructive habits
and won't get help, you must prioritize
your own health and well-being.**

Taking care of yourself will go a long way in helping you care for your parents. Find ways to empathize with them and encourage them, being careful not to nag. Informed empathy is more credible and appreciated than sales-oriented "feel good" statements that patronize our parents and undermine their concerns. Determine what activities they are still able to carry on, and then help them do so. Enjoy the ups of the roller coaster, and stay positive when the downtimes inevitably roll around. But understand that you ultimately cannot change your parents' attitudes or behaviors. By taking care of yourself and maintaining a positive outlook, you and your immediate family still will be much better off for your efforts.

The Caregivers' Own Emotional Roller Coaster

Another Wild Ride

The emotional roller coaster of aging challenges the caregivers as much as your parents. It adds complexities and surprises to "family life as usual," making the twists and turns and ups and downs feel unbearable at times. In hindsight, the biggest surprise was the length of the ride, even though our experiences were vastly different.

In one case, the caregiving process developed slowly and naturally—making helpful suggestions to Mom and Dad here and there and offering assistance in little ways that felt manageable but still helpful. Over several years, this pattern gradually increased until the milestone decision was finally made for a major downsize and relocation. In the other case, the process began instantly with a severe, unexpected stroke. (But then again, aren't all strokes unexpected?) In each of our experiences, we made life-changing decisions for (and with) our parents after researching numerous alternatives and prayerfully doing our best.

Once the big decisions were made, however, we naively expected circumstances to improve and our lives to "get back to normal." Little did we realize at the time that we had climbed onto a roller-coaster ride that we'd stay on until our parents were gone. For sure, life improved at times. Sometimes, those quieter periods lasted several years. Other times, they were unexpectedly short, lasting only a few months. But in any case, another situation was sure to pop up and shift things around once again.

Similar to the range of emotions experienced by the parents, the caregivers undergo their own set of highs and lows, one often dovetailing into another:

* **Low:** The unwelcome burden of realizing for the first time that your parents can't do everything for themselves anymore, and they really need your help.
* **High:** The satisfaction of seeing your parents' appreciation for small, helpful tasks.
* **Low:** The frustration when you can't quickly identify and find the caregiving solutions that you anticipated.
* **High:** The delight of finding acceptable and affordable options in the right location.
* **Low:** The discouragement of discovering that none of your options are acceptable or affordable from your parents' perspective.
* **High:** The relief of finding an agreeable solution for all (even if it's a reluctant agreement).
* **High:** The comfort of seeing things work out and embarking upon a new pattern of life that meets everyone's major needs.
* **Low:** The distress and guilt when your immediate family members (either a spouse or kids still at home) are unhappy with the new arrangements and have to make changes to accommodate the aging parents.
* **Low:** The annoyance of dealing with siblings who are dissatisfied with the hard-to-achieve arrangements, especially when they're unwilling to help—physically, financially, or even emotionally.
* **High:** The joy of a friend or loved one's realization that you really need a hand, and then jumping in to help.

* **Low:** The renewed discouragement of realizing that the current solution, once again, no longer meets your parents' needs and another arrangement is needed—fast!
* **Low:** The resigned feeling of recognizing that this process is a cycle—and it's stuck on *repeat*!
* **High:** The peace and comfort of finally accepting the long-term nature of your role as the caregiver in this cycle.
* **High:** The enjoyment of being able to laugh at yourself and the circumstances—especially the moments when everyone can laugh together.
* **High:** The satisfaction of overcoming the setbacks and little annoyances more easily each time, eventually accepting them as part of life.
* **High:** The contentment of looking back, after your parents have passed away, knowing that you did what you could to enhance their final years with love and joy.

> **The caregiver's highs and lows are always changing, moving back and forth along the spectrum of emotions. Who ever thought it would be static?**

The roller-coaster emotions that come with aging parents, whether or not you are providing care for them, have surprised many adult children—ourselves included. For years, you enjoy the luxury of watching your kids grow steadily more independent until the day you finally become carefree empty nesters. You rarely think about, much less worry about, your parents. Suddenly, in what seems like an overnight change, their habits make an alarming shift. You notice they're spending retirement savings on unnecessary stuff in catalogs or the Internet. Or perhaps they're giving it away to con artists or in philanthropic gifts for dubious purposes. You begin to worry whether they're taking all of their medicine at the proper times and in the proper amounts (and believe us, they probably aren't). Questions you'd never considered before regularly pop into your minds:

* Should they still be driving?
* Can they live on their own?
* Will they outlive their financial resources? Will we need to support them?
* Are they taking their medicine?
* What if they fall or are injured and there is nobody to hear them cry for help?
* What is my responsibility? Will they think I'm meddling?
* Can I handle them on my own? How?

Most of us are used to depending on our parents—not the other way around! When we were stressed and needed encouragement or help, we could pick up the phone or go visit Mom and Dad. Their stability and life experience helped calm us and counsel us. But as our parents age, conversations become different. Rather than being the listening audience, they rattle off frequent recitations of their own bodily malfunctions, such as:

* My doctor says my heart is in arrhythmia.
* I'm so constipated. I just can't eat meat like I used to.
* I'm always short of breath. Do you think that means I have fluid in my lungs? Or is it COPD?
* What? I can't hear you; why don't you speak up?

* Why don't people use bigger print? I can never read the instructions. Oh well, I probably don't need to read them anyway. I'm pretty sure that I know what needs to be done.

As our parents age, we experience emotions that we have never associated with them before, such as anxiety, frustration, grief, loss, fear, helplessness, and dread, among many others. At least initially, these worrisome emotions seem to dominate our feelings, and we want to shoo them away.

**We realize now that our initial caregiving
concerns about our parents,
were an excellent start. Though
stressful, they led us to address
the most pressing issue first, followed
by the next one, and the next.
Each time, we discovered growing
degrees of competency and
satisfaction as we climbed the wall
of worry one step at a time.**

Having an advisor or a guide who has already lived through this process provides some much-needed comfort. It helps just knowing that these normal reactions and responses will subsequently allow us to regain control of our lives. We don't have to give in to the overwhelming feelings of inadequacy. Despite these new challenges, we can also expect new experiences full of joy and hope.

Finding the New Normal

Ben and Jill, two twenty-two-year-olds, were married for five months when Jill's father was diagnosed with an aggressive form of brain cancer at the young age of forty-five. Six months later, they stood by an open grave, mourning his death. They had no idea what to do or how to handle the powerful emotions of fear, loss, helplessness and grief. They felt like they were plunging headfirst down a hill with no rails or brakes. They simply leaned on each other, prayed, and marched on. In time Ben and Jill found a new normal. Jill's mother remarried, and the young couple had their own kids to focus on.

Thirty-five years later, their two daughters were married and independent, so Ben and Jill relocated to a new town, a new house, and new jobs. They had deliberately made all these changes to step off the big-city treadmill and reclaim sanity in their lives. They planned to slow down, simplify, and reclaim their mental and physical health. Three months into this new and idyllic life, they received a call: Jill's mother, Martha, was in the hospital. "She seems to have had a stroke," the caller said. "The doctors are concerned."

The idyll was over, and reality set in. Recalling their only prior experience of this nature, they reacted quickly with no second thoughts and began taking steps to help. Only later did they recognize that some adjustments and sacrifices would need to be made and that another new normal status was evolving.

Against all odds, the stroke had no serious impact on Martha's immediate health or mental functioning. She spent one week in the hospital, and then a week with Jill and Ben in their new home. When Martha returned to her home, everyone was optimistic. It looked like things would return to normal with little disruption of anyone's life. Ben and Jill felt a great sense of joy and relief about Martha's recovery and anticipated a quick return to their own "life plan."

Four days after Martha's successful return home, Ben's phone rang again. It was Jill's uncle, who lived near Martha and frequently checked on her. "She's had another stroke," the uncle said. "She's lost consciousness and is on her way to the hospital."

This second stroke changed everything. Martha would never live on her own again. She lost both physical and mental functions. During her stay in the hospital, Ben and Jill realized that their new normal would now include Martha living in a facility that would provide the care she needed. After leaving the hospital, Martha entered rehab for one hundred days (the Medicare limit for a rehabilitation stay.) Ben and Jill moved her from the rehab center to an assisted-living facility. She could no longer talk. She could only occasionally sign her name. She answered questions correctly only about 20 to 30 percent of the time. Yet every time she saw her daughter, she was able to communicate her frustration that she couldn't go home. So the new normal on Ben and Jill's roller-coaster ride now included new personal sacrifices and unexpected financial constraints, all compounded by Martha's sorrow and anger. On top of everything, Ben and Jill were also caring for Martha's husband and trying to make time for their own daughters and their families.

Six months after this cataclysmic stroke, Martha's husband died. Though Ben and Jill had planned for a calmer, less-anxious life, each drastic set of turns eroded their "new normal" once again. Nevertheless, they adapted. They made the necessary adjustments as they adapted to each shift to another "new normal." They still celebrated important events in their own lives and their daughters' lives and found contentment and satisfaction in unexpected places and opportunities.

Living Together?

Paige's mom, Bev, had Alzheimer's but a strong physical constitution. Although weak from congestive heart failure, her dad, Ted, still had excellent cognitive abilities. When he called Paige and told her that he needed help with Bev, Paige and her husband agreed to move her parents into their own home. The bulk of this life adjustment rested with Paige since she did not work out of the home and was primarily involved in volunteer work. But the living arrangements were feasible and acceptable for everyone. Ted continued handling many of his and Bev's daily living activities. They were even able to look after the house when Paige and her husband went on short weekend trips.

Although Paige's life became a lot more hectic with running her parents around, this arrangement worked well for several years, despite several timing and organizational challenges. Besides taking care of her parents' transportation needs, Paige also took care of their physical housekeeping and nourishment. She soon found some relief in elder day care and elder in-home companion care, but even that required additional transportation and scheduling. Despite periodic spats and disagreements that arose from living together, Paige's relationship with her parents grew stronger. She learned much about her parents' backgrounds, their childhoods, and their families that she had never known. Her experiences even stimulated a newfound interest in genealogy, which gave Ted ample opportunity to reminisce, drawing Paige and her parents closer together.

After several fulfilling years of this new normal, Bev's Alzheimer's related behavior slowly became more obvious and harder to deal with. She needed more assistance in ways that Paige was not prepared to handle. So Paige began to research assisted-living facilities within easy driving distance of her home. Beginning with ratings and guidance from both state and private websites, she became aware of the differences in services and costs.

Once Paige and her husband began visiting those facilities that seemed good on paper, they quickly learned that their physical appearance and cleanliness varied quite a bit. Some facilities had nursing and housekeeping staffs who seemed to genuinely enjoy their jobs and really cared for the elderly in their facilities. Others didn't appear to care nearly as much. Finding a match that looked good according to state-recommended health, cleanliness, and care metrics that also felt warm and friendly often appeared impossible, causing great frustration. Add to that a strong desire for the facility to be close enough to encourage regular visits, and Paige became pessimistic about finding a solution. In time, however, she was able to locate a facility that seemed to meet her parents' needs at an affordable cost.

But now she was met by another unexpected complication. There was a waiting list with an unpredictable length of time until a vacancy occurred. The unpredictability of vacancies was due to the unpredictability of seniors' move-out dates, which usually occurred when they moved to a hospital or a nursing home to receive additional care. Paige was disappointed, but, after some discussion, she added her parents' names to the waiting list, anticipating a lengthy delay. To everyone's surprise, the waiting list cleared within several months, and a vacancy came up much more quickly than expected.

When Paige learned of the opening, it had to be accepted quickly (in less than a week), or the opening would be passed on to the next name on the waiting list. With the support of friends, Paige's family accepted the vacancy, signed the contract, loaded Ted and Bev's important belongings into a moving van, and immediately relocated them to the nearby assisted-living facility (about twenty miles away). Unlike the original move across several states when Ted and Bev moved into Paige's home, this transition was easily accomplished and done somewhat incrementally. After only a few days, things improved significantly, giving Paige needed contentment and peace.

Things worked out even better when Ted and Bev quickly adapted to their new surroundings in a small suite with a living area, one bedroom, one bath, and no kitchen. Residents ate together in a dining room with several lounge and break areas where volunteers provided periodic entertainment.

Once again, life was good. This new normal meant fewer day-to-day tasks for Paige but also increased her travel and out-of-pocket costs substantially. Less housekeeping. Less hassle. A safer environment for her parents. The only downside was the additional time spent driving between home and the facility. She had to plan for an extra hour or more before and after their doctor's appointments, errands, or other visits. But the assisted-living facility handled the laundry, the housekeeping, most meals, and daily assistance. Overall, Paige made the adjustment quickly and easily and felt greatly relieved.

For the next two years, the weekly routine worked well for everyone. For holidays and special events, Paige or her husband brought her parents home for family time, especially when their kids and newly arrived grandkids were visiting.

Eventually, Ted had to move to the hospital for some emergency care. Without Ted, Bev could not live alone with her Alzheimer's, even in assisted living. Fortunately, during the two-year lull in activity, Paige had methodically and patiently located an Alzheimer's home nearby that also had an affiliated nursing home with it. She easily moved her mother there with no hassle and also moved her parent's belongings out of the assisted-living facility. Due to the never-ending waiting list for assisted living, this move again had to be done quickly to make room for new residents. But this time Paige and her family were prepared, so it went smoothly.

When Ted's health recovered sufficiently to be discharged from the hospital, he needed some rehabilitation. So he moved into the nursing home by Bev's Alzheimer's home. In this new environment, with Ted and Bev in different facilities, Ted always asked about Bev, so Paige periodically took him to see her. Bev sometimes asked about Ted, too, but she was usually quickly distracted by other things. Although her parents were steadily losing their physical health, this was a period of relative calmness without many crises occurring. As a result, it was a period of peace, stability, and reflection for Paige and her family.

After a couple of years, Ted passed away. Bev remained in the Alzheimer's home for another year until she had a medical emergency that required a hospital stay. Afterward, she went through rehab and moved into a nursing home just three miles from Paige's home. In this final arrangement, Paige visited regularly and was able to be with her mother, sharing her love and devotion without undue frustrations or minor emergencies until the end. After two more years, Bev passed away too.

**Caregiving solutions are never
ideal, never permanent, and
never attained without investment
of time, energy, and money.
But those investments create
tomorrow's memories!**

Surviving the Roller Coaster

As should be obvious from these vignettes, the caregiving process is truly a roller coaster of events and emotions. With mixed feelings about the various levels of care, time, and costs involved, viable solutions often felt out of reach. But ultimately, these caregivers always found a way to make things work. The solutions were never ideal, happily-ever-after propositions. Money was scarce. Time was required. Sacrifices were made. Few decisions were easy and quick to be accepted by all. In addition, throughout each drawn-out process, the parents' physical, mental, and emotional capabilities were steadily eroding, and solutions that were safe, acceptable, and beneficial were constantly changing and evolving. Worries and hand-wringing about the right decisions sometimes plagued both the caregivers and the parents. But along the winding path, big and small successes could also be recognized and celebrated, spawning joy.

The apostle Paul noted in his biblical letter to the Philippians (Phil. 4:12), "I have learned the secret of being content in any and every situation, whether well fed or hungry, whether living in plenty or in want." That level of contentment cannot come when the caregiver focuses solely on what has been lost and what has gone wrong. However, there must be an honest appraisal of our current situation. Consider these suggestions:

1. **Allow yourself to feel pain and to grieve.** When first experiencing parental decline and loss, we had no idea how to process our feelings or deal with the death of a parent. In our later years, as we experienced our parents' decline firsthand and began providing some of their care, we learned the importance of recognizing and accepting our feelings. It still wasn't easy or natural for us. It took time and effort and, sometimes, assistance from a professional counselor to become more comfortable with our emotions as our circumstances spun out of our control. We allowed ourselves to feel the pain and heartache of watching our parents suffer and live diminished lives. We also allowed ourselves to grieve the loss of our own plans and adjust our expectations about the life we had wanted for ourselves. But the grieving should not remain the primary focus! Recognize and feel the pain, but, at some point, we must learn to accept each stage of "new normal" and put the past in the rearview mirror. The grief may still bubble up at times, but we must refuse to let it dominate our lives. If necessary, it is totally appropriate to make a promise to our families and ourselves to make up for the sacrifices when we get the chance. That promise will appropriately focus our attention on the future and, as a result, also avoids continuing any focus on the grief over what could have been.

2. **Ask for help.** We both came from families who modeled self-sufficiency and self-reliance. If we had problems, we worked harder and silently marched on. Growing up in that environment gave us each the natural inclination and wherewithal to

try to handle adversity alone. So when a parent had a stroke, our first reaction was to keep it to ourselves and deal with it. Fortunately, we soon gave up on that unrealistic idea of self-reliance. The burden and trauma were just too much. The pain would swallow us whole if we didn't have someone to keep us from sinking into the sea of self-pity and despair. We relied on doctors, nurses, clinicians, friends, family, co-workers, church members, and anyone we could find who had been through similar experiences. Sharing sorrow cuts it in half, or at least makes it manageable. And when inter-acting with others who have lived through similar situations and survived, we can see hope and opportunity beyond the immediate crisis.

3. **Bolster the caregiver.** Taking care of aging parents, even in "normal situations," is challenging! But dealing with ag-ing parents who are undergoing some physical, emotional, relational, or financial trauma can be totally debilitating. Especially in today's world, it is too easy to become cyni-cal, skeptical, and pessimistic. But those attitudes are defi-nitely not helpful in these situations and can even become the beginnings of friction between caregivers. If we become incapacitated due to poor health or a lousy attitude or any other reason, we are unable to do any good for those who depend on us, whether it's our parents or our other fam-ily members. We must try to maintain good health as well as a good attitude to be of any use to anyone. Therefore, this is truly an important consideration. Take time and ef-fort to reward yourself and feel good on a regular basis. If there are others also involved in the caregiving process with us, we should also encourage and stimulate them. With the help of a counselor, we learned the importance of extending

goodwill toward those caregivers (a spouse or sibling, most often) as well as toward ourselves. A good rule of thumb is to regularly ask, "What does support and satisfaction look like to you? What can I do to help you? What can I do to bring some near-term joy into your life?" Then find a way to provide it.

4. **Find new things to celebrate.** Celebrating a few small victories each day can sustain us through obstacles and help us avoid wading into cynicism and pessimism. We celebrated the ability to sign a name and to eat with a fork with a non-dominant hand. We found joy in being able to walk down a hallway unaided. Sometimes, there is even satisfaction in having a good hair day. Remember? We celebrated similar events when our children were infants and toddlers. Now when we adjust our expectations, we can also find joy in the smaller accomplishments. Focus on what's possible, not what has been lost.

   We also tried to simply love our parents for who they were and not for what they could accomplish or do for us. We found honor in being a child or child-in-law and returning the care our parents had provided for us as children.

5) **Actively seek wisdom and clarity in decisions, including prayer.** Fear of not knowing what to do or what the "right" decisions were often accelerated the roller coaster of emotions. On our emotional ride to places we had never been, we sometimes felt like our decisions were matters of life and death. (On one occasion, we spent several days worrying over which box to check on the do-not-resuscitate form.) We found wisdom and reassurance in asking wise and godly people for prayers, guidance, and clarity for the decisions we faced.

It is emotional and stressful to watch people we love go through trauma and decline. When we accept the impact of this reality and turn outside ourselves for support, we find it easier to experience peace and joy. Rather than denying or fighting our parents' aging process, we want to join them in walking through it. When we did, we discovered tenderness, mercy, comfort, and joy in little things that we never expected. You can too!

Chapter 5

Coming to Grips with Continuing Transitions and Mortality

Supporting a Surviving Spouse

The Loneliness of Survival

If your parents are still married—to one another or to a different partner—you will probably help at least one of them through the death of a spouse. Despite the vast differences caretakers face with their parents physically, financially, and emotionally, most people confront this situation at some point.

Immediately after the funeral, as life returns to a daily rhythm, watch for the loneliness and associated depression of survivors.

Providing your parents with emotional support, helpful assistance, and serious companionship will go a long way to strengthen your relationship for the future. Your relationship will evolve and change after the death of a spouse. Sometimes that change will be a positive one, but often, it will be an uncomfortable one. Some of the challenging situations that a surviving parent faces include the following:

* Extreme loneliness and depression
* The pressure of handling all the responsibilities previously managed by the other spouse
* A lack of purpose (usually following a short period of initial relief), especially if the surviving parent had been a primary caregiver
* An inability or aversion to living alone

We need to immediately become aware of the survivor's loneliness and associated depression and provide assistance quickly, without waiting to be asked. Providing your surviving parent with ongoing emotional and physical help with regular tasks and being available more often for day-to-day companionship will go a long ways toward addressing the challenges involved in losing a spouse. In most cases, surviving spouses will initially be busy making funeral arrangements. Subsequently they will be involved in settling the estate for a period of time. That required level of activity will help keep them busy and take their minds off the immediate grief, although there will naturally be many sad times. That period of high levels of activity also gives the caregivers a chance to plan for the longer term (that is, after the activity subsides).

Driven by necessity, new patterns of life will quickly emerge for the survivor. Observant caregivers should also recognize the need for new patterns of their own involvement and put a plan into place as soon as possible. As much as practical, involve family and friends, since they usually want to help but are typically focused on providing desserts and casseroles for the first week or two. That attention and concern is definitely welcomed, but companionship and support in the coming few months is equally valuable, if not more so. The continuing support is also harder to maintain and absolutely will not happen without a stimulus and organizer to encourage it. Combining some social time with performance of minor housekeeping or financial tasks will simultaneously address multiple situations mentioned above. It will provide a transition period into the longer-term period of living alone without a spouse.

Since survivors are exceptionally vulnerable, they often solve the problem of loneliness themselves—through remarriage or a live-in partner. While this will probably feel shocking or even painful to the caregiver, it should certainly not be unexpected, and it can frequently be exactly what's needed. Despite the potential of a new person taking advantage of the surviving parent, a compatible companion is often an excellent solution. Even if a new relationship is not everything that was anticipated, desired, or favored, it can nevertheless offer your parent the tremendous benefits of comfort, caring companionship, and partnership in the burden of daily tasks. In the long run, this will help you too.

If a relationship with a new partner occurs (and it may happen whether we support the idea or not), the potential for intrafamily competition, jealousy, and even hostility can easily result in estrangement between the surviving parent and the rest of the family. That estrangement will consume far more time and resources than the comparable effort of providing immediate support. The resulting competition for memories, memorabilia, family heirlooms, and legacy items will compound the hostility and deepen the estrangement. So devoting additional attention to the relationship with the surviving spouse will be an excellent investment of your time, paying many dividends over the years. Furthermore if a remarriage is in the cards, it is better to accept and embrace a new parental partner, despite the natural initial reluctance, than it will be to begin a lengthy competition or a hostile relationship with them. The new partner is there on a daily basis and will always be able to have the last word and weigh in after the caregiver has left.

Even if you graciously accept a new partner or spouse, be prepared for significant changes that person will bring to the daily life and environment of your surviving parent. The new couple will not want to live with the arrangements of your deceased parent, not wanting to face those memories day after day. So some things may be cast aside that you may view as important and meaningful memorabilia. Inconsiderate or inadvertent disposal of these items can create as much friction as the marriage itself. But it's important to keep in mind that once estrangement occurs, rebuilding the relationship is not always possible. This topic could easily consume an entire book by itself, but we will only touch on it here. Remember that, in the end, you probably care more about your relationship with your parent than the family heirlooms, memorabilia, and other stuff you may be arguing about.

**Since most of us love our parents and
want to be sources of comfort
(and not antagonism and stress), be
considerate toward them as
they find their way through the grief and loss.**

We only get one chance to do this. When we support them with our time, assistance, understanding, and patience—even if we do not agree with all their decisions and lifestyle choices—we make a valuable investment in a long-term continuing relationship with our surviving parent.

Reading Between the Lines

During the eighteen months after Clark's mom died, his dad Kirk moved out of the family home where he and his wife had lived for more than thirty years. Kirk seemed to adjust well to life in his new home and stayed busy giving stimulating history lectures at a local museum. Although Clark lived a day's drive away, he tried to stay actively involved in his dad's life through regular phone calls and visits once or twice a year. When Kirk made a week-long trip to visit Clark and his family, they had several opportunities for meaningful discussions.

One day, when they were returning from an errand, Kirk asked, "Have I told you I'm hiring an assistant?"

"An assistant?" Clark replied, somewhat surprised. "Why do you need an assistant?"

"I need help with typing and bookkeeping," Kirk said, "and I also want to write my memoirs."

That made sense to Clark and answered his primary question. After a few minutes of further discussion, they arrived home and went inside to eat, ending the conversation that day.

The next day, they were running errands again, and Kirk volunteered, "I plan to have my assistant live with me."

Naively, Clark asked why.

"Because it will be easier to work together, and it makes economic sense." Kirk said. "I have the extra bedroom downstairs, so my assistant will save the amount of the monthly rent, which is quite a bit of money."

Again, after another short discussion, they once again arrived at home and ended the conversation. Later at dinner, Clark mentioned to his wife, "Has dad told you that he's hiring an assistant?"

"Why no," Clark's wife said. Looking to Kirk, she innocently asked, "What will an assistant do?"

Kirk started to reply, "Well, she—"

"She?" Clark exploded. "What do you mean *she*? You never told me your assistant was a woman."

"I didn't?" Kirk asked sheepishly. "I'm sorry."

After further investigation, Clark discovered that Kirk had known his new assistant for only about a month and had met her through his museum lectures. Two days after returning home, Kirk called and announced that he and his new "assistant" were getting married in a few weeks. Though Clark should have asked deeper questions from the start, he also could not have changed the situation no matter what he did.

Later, Clark learned that Kirk had felt deeply alone after his wife of forty-three years (Clark's mom) had passed away. Prior to meeting his new wife, Kirk had also sought to reconnect with an old girlfriend from fifty years earlier. He clearly needed companionship and maybe even a helper to a much greater degree than Clark realized. Clark's wife and daughter readily accepted Kirk's new wife, but Clark and his new stepmom had a stormy relationship for several years (which, in hindsight, Clark allowed to go on too long). Finally, Clark realized that he was not winning the battle for the heart and mind of his dad. Not wanting to be estranged from him, he reached out to his new stepmom and eventually made peace with her. After that, they had several peaceful years and ultimately got along very well.

After several years, Clark eventually realized that Kirk's life was happy and fulfilled with his new wife. They were married seventeen years before Kirk passed away. His younger wife took excellent care of Kirk and always kept Clark informed, thereby eliminating Clark's concerns about Kirk living a safe and active life halfway across the country.

After Kirk passed away, Clark and his stepmom continued to have a good relationship.

The Survivor's Dilemma

When Dan passed away unexpectedly, his wife, Jenn, was left with their house and an annuity based on Dan's prior income and employment. Within a year, she sold the house to relocate a few miles away where she could live inexpensively and enjoy the outdoors and her horses. But she had some acreage that took lots of work to maintain. She soon found that a single neighbor, Owen, was friendly and compatible. He often helped with chores around her property and was willing to take care of the horses when Jenn was out of town. Before long, Jenn and Owen were talking about marriage. But Jenn's annuity, which they needed to make ends meet, would be terminated if she remarried. So Jenn and Owen moved in together and did not marry. Dan's son was morally against Jenn's decision and tried to dissuade her. But he could not come up with any alternatives, so Jenn and Owen continued with their plans.

This situation is common, often because of financial restrictions, as in this vignette. A source of income, insurance coverage, or assets (such as a house) is frequently dependent on the survivor remaining single and not remarrying. Many people of retirement age quietly live together, married in every way except legally. Better retirement planning could help protect the income of a spouse who may want to remarry one day. The children of the deceased spouse should provide support when possible.

Despite his discomfort with the situation, Dan's son eventually accepted Jenn's decision. Our parents' decisions are often beyond our control or influence. We have to decide if asserting our belief and dissatisfaction is worth the price of estrangement. It usually isn't.

The Wrong Sequence Creates Melancholy Results

Fred retired and relocated to a retirement community with his wife, Olive. They went through a long, painful downsizing as they moved into a modest two-bedroom home. It was just right for their needs and also included a small extra bedroom. Their sons lived in a metroplex five hundred miles away. Since Fred was eight years older than Olive and demographics indicate that women live longer than men, both of them always anticipated that Olive would outlive Fred.

After a few years, they both lost their ability to drive, almost simultaneously. Then a few months afterward, Olive unexpectedly passed away first. Fred was devastated. During the immediate period prior to Olive's passing and the first weeks afterward, his sons took turns visiting him, both with and without his grandchildren. They provided lots of needed help as well as close companionship, but neither could visit as much as desired. Fred's friends and neighbors also helped out with companionship and assistance in a variety of daily tasks as well as one-time issues associated with Olive's passing. He had insightfully purchased long-term-care insurance a decade earlier, so he was able to take advantage of an in-home care companion.

Nevertheless, Fred was by himself most of the time. After decades of living with Olive as his daily companion and confidante, the loneliness was overwhelming. It was compounded by the fact that Olive had always paid the bills, handled the investments, and filed the insurance paperwork. So Fred's loneliness was worsened by the frustration of trying to grasp the timing and nature of all the tasks that Olive had performed for years.

This situation illustrates virtually all the despondence and frustration associated with the death of a spouse. The sorrow of Olive's passing was heightened by Fred's resulting loneliness, lack of purpose, and inefficiency in handling tasks performed by Olive. Sadly, this situation is all too common. Preparation should be made years in advance for backing up tasks typically performed exclusively by one half of a marital partnership. As mentioned throughout these sections, we should all take responsibility for assuring regular contact with friends and family in order to avoid turning a sorrowful result into a melancholy existence.

Looking for a Loved One

Beth's parents had lived nearby in an assisted-living home for several years. Although Beth's dad was frail, he had a sound mind and was able to maintain their affairs reasonably well. But Beth's mother, Alice, had Alzheimer's. Despite the fact that we sometimes despair over those with Alzheimer's, their needs are often simple, and they are emotionally content as long as no one upsets them. When Alice's brother passed away, Beth made the mistake of telling her about the loss, which was very upsetting for Alice. Though she no longer remembered her brother's passing shortly afterward, she still felt upset. She just didn't know why. Based on this experience, when Beth's dad passed away a few years later, she decided not to tell Alice. Though they didn't want to lie to Alice, the situation worked itself out. Whenever Alice asked about him, Beth and her family quickly learned to defer her questions with the response, "Where did you see him last?" Alice usually decided that she had last seen him preparing a meal or chopping wood or taking care of some other chore. After a few minutes of looking for him, she forgot about it due to her Alzheimer's related memory losses. Protecting Alice's emotions in this way supported her mental condition and was definitely easier on Beth, her family, and the caregivers at the facility—a win-win situation for all.

Freedom or Emptiness?

When her husband of more than forty years passed away, Cheryl initially felt great relief. She had been his sole caregiver for a decade during his bout with Alzheimer's. Even after settling him in a home for Alzheimer's patients, she still visited daily and managed their affairs. She never took trips or visited family in other cities because she didn't want to leave him. After he passed away and his affairs were put in order, Cheryl had time to do many of the things she had been unable to do. She was free! With her caregiving sensibilities, she soon volunteered to stay with her sister-in-law and her husband for a week to give their own caregivers a break. That enabled her to take an airplane trip for the first time in her life. She felt fulfilled by the help she provided, relieving her niece of daily caregiving responsibilities for a few days.

Once she returned home to her new "normal," there were long periods of solitude and loneliness. She had no hobbies or casual interests because she had devoted most of her retirement years to being her husband's caregiver. Although she had some interest in travel, she was reluctant to do so because of health concerns. Rather than being free, Cheryl's life was empty. She had no children, so no one came regularly to visit, help out, or socialize. After a couple of years, Cheryl's brother talked her into selling her house and moving into assisted living, where she had a short period of greater social interaction. But in less than six months, she became ill and passed away.

This sad situation is all too common. The long-anticipated retirement and freedom never materialize. Especially after the loss of a spouse, "freedom" morphs into an extended period of emptiness. Without family for encouragement, there is no one to interact with or to discuss and explore interesting topics and alternatives. There must be a special place in heaven for compassionate souls who recognize these symptoms in a lonely elderly person and offer some assistance, companionship, and purpose.

Those with surviving parents should be motivated to actively get involved in their lives for their remaining time, whether

**months, years, or decades. Why not
also be alert for other lonely
seniors in your path who could
use some encouragement?**

Despite the example of the vignette above, in our own experience, women deal better with the aftereffects of survival than men. Women typically have support groups where members look out for one another and take care of those in their groups who are hurting in any way—physically or emotionally. The typical male does not want to appear to be vulnerable, so he withdraws and become isolated—in his man cave, by reading, by watching sports on TV, and in many other ways. Men just aren't prone to reaching to one another to help others "feel better." That just wouldn't be very manly.

As noted in earlier sections, time spent with your parents after the death of a spouse will be time well-spent. Despite inevitable challenges and disagreements, your relationship will grow in unexpected ways, and you will create new memories.

Looking to the Future

During the weeks and months after a parent passes away, one of two things will happen: you and your surviving parent will either come together, or you will grow apart. There will be some measure of increased stress and loneliness in almost any situation of loss. Take advantage of this delicate time period without being too insistent that your loved ones take your suggestions. Taking time to listen and understand their concerns can result in a more fulfilling relationship for their remaining time. In doing this, you may help them avoid withering away in loneliness or quickly remarrying for the desired companionship.

Regardless of your parents' choices, you must find a difficult balance: staying active in their lives while allowing them to make their own decisions. This approach will help you avoid estrangement over differences.

Also, this grieving period is a good time to reassess many of the topics of earlier chapters—from the new perspective of having a single parent going through the aging process. Some of the previous decisions will still apply, but some will change. Since survivors must deal with the belongings of the deceased partner (both memorabilia as well as just "stuff"), this is an excellent opportunity to help them and spend time with them in another round of downsizing. But we must be sensitive to their feelings about these personal effects and the memories they represent. Watch for opportunities to engage your parent's memories, openness, and ideas through new discussions that may never have occurred any other way. A patient willingness to listen to and gently inquire of your surviving parent will pay great dividends—now and in the long run. Understanding your parent's hopes, desires, and preferences will be useful many times in future years. Embrace these opportunities!

The Spiral of Lost Capabilities

Undesired Transitions

As noted in earlier chapters, the statistics are overwhelming—most people want to grow older in their own homes. They don't want to end up in assisted-living or nursing homes. They want to pass from this world at home. But the reality is different from what we want it to be: more than 70 percent of seniors die in hospitals. The large discrepancy between what we want and what actually happens highlights the truth about aging—as we grow older, we gradually lose our capabilities.

Furthermore, although 90 percent of seniors want to have meaningful, end-of-life discussions with their family, only 30 percent have actually had them. These are equally astounding statistics. In our anecdotal experience, many seniors freely and openly discuss their own loss of capabilities with their friends of comparable ages. Apparently, they really do understand the impending progressive loss of capabilities. However, they also want to hold onto their freedom and independence as long as possible, often well past the point of common sense and safety. Parents often worry that their family will want to move them into a senior-care facility before they are ready to go, just to make it "easier" on everybody. Of course, some seniors staunchly insist on remaining in their homes under any circumstances, causing their children and family members to live in constant anxiety and fear of an emergency phone call. Such crises often expose the children's ignorance of their parents' affairs and desires.

It's easier to collaborate on a strategic plan for aging when adult children talk with their parents about the expectations involved in the transition.

Just like our children progressively mature and gain physical, intellectual, and emotional capabilities over time, most seniors also lose their adult capabilities gradually—that is, they don't lose them overnight. There are many different models of this process. But overall, the losses come roughly in the inverse order that those capabilities were gained years earlier as children. From normal middle-aged adulthood (usually beginning in our fifties), we pass through several "senior-living" phases, loosely characterized as independence, vulnerability, dependence, and end-of-life.[10] Two major differences from the model of capabilities gained by children through their growth phases are the following:

(1) The senior-living phases are not as closely tied to our actual age.
(2) Not everyone encounters all the same phenomena during the aging process.

There are definitely, however, distinct phases that are encountered by most aging seniors. These phases may be generally summarized as follows:

Independence: Extended free time (even if still working)
                  Eligible for retirement benefits
                  Limited degradation of capabilities

---

10 www.personalfutures.net/id65.html

Some medications
Continuing interest in and awareness of
external events
Generally positive outlook
Able to live alone or with a partner

Vulnerability:
Little or no work-oriented activities
Onset of physical frailty
Significantly reduced energy level
Noticeable, periodic, cognitive chal-
lenges
Increasing health or well-being issues
Increasing medications
Awareness or frustration with aging and
capability loss
Waning interest in external events
Some assisted-living care may be needed

Dependence:
Needs help with daily personal functions
Significant frailty
Possible dementia
Interrelated health issues with complex
medications
Little or no interest in external events
Frequent negative outlook
Probable need for assisted-living or
nursing care

End-of-Life
Terminal condition(s)
Likely hospitalization or hospice care

The first three of these phases can vary from months to decades in length and often overlap as we morph from one phase to another. Depending on individual health and environment, any particular person may or may not exhibit all these characteristics. For example, many octogenarians with frail bodies still have sharp minds and retain a curiosity and interest in external affairs, contributing valuable perspectives and insights into world or national affairs, investment options, sports history, or many other areas of interest. Similarly, many who are healthy and fit but with varying degrees of dementia are still perfectly capable of participating in sports activities, but they may need help in keeping score or remembering whose turn it is.

Despite the many differences, the steady loss of our capabilities causes much frustration, especially in those who have been used to being "the rocks" in their families for decades. Seniors often cope with these losses by cracking jokes about "senior moments" or incontinence that can surprise or shock us. Since our aging parents live with these conditions and confront them on a daily basis, they are often more willing to accept the deterioration than we are.

When an unexpected debilitating event occurs, be ready to step in with a helping hand and a supportive attitude. Then expect to encounter escalating needs and a likely transition to assisted living or nursing care in the future.

The pace of change varies with the individual, but transitions often take shorter periods of time than anticipated at the outset. For that reason, once you begin to investigate the pros and cons of available options, it's important to stay in contact with viable and competent providers. Increased care will most likely be needed sooner rather than later.

One Best-Case Scenario

Dan lived a fulfilling life in the twenty years after his wife of forty-five years passed away. He remarried less than two years afterward, was active in the local retirees' community, and lectured regularly about historical events that he had experienced. For more than ten years, he traveled significantly throughout the United States and made regular returns to his roots in Europe. His second wife, Jenn, was a big help with Dan's activities, driving him places and supporting his involvement with his local community and family. When Dan was in his late eighties, he stopped driving altogether since his reflexes were naturally slowing and his sensory acuity was eroding. But with Jenn's help, he continued mentoring, teaching, and participating in activities that kept his mind engaged even as his body slowed down.

During this period, Dan had two hip replacements as well as several lesser surgeries, always bouncing back, although the bounce-back periods took longer each time. For each of these recovery periods, he went to rehab centers as long as necessary and was determined to get back to normal. With the help of therapy and encouragement from his friends, he always emerged in good spirits and in surprisingly good physical health, quickly returning to his prior lifestyle.

Jenn helped Dan's health immensely when she got him a dog— a Pomeranian named Pooh. The dog was small enough that Dan had no problems controlling him and walking him on a leash, so Jenn insisted he take Pooh for regular walks several times a day. Life was good.

Then Dan had a minor stroke. He lost some use of his right arm, and his speech was slurred, but specialists thought it was recoverable with therapy. Just like he'd done for his previous surgeries, Dan went to a rehab center and began the recovery process. Though the stroke was more challenging to overcome, Dan's prior successes and continued encouragement from loved ones helped him continue the hard work. Jenn also worked hard to motivate him when he got tired or discouraged.

The unwavering adoration of Pooh became a major factor in Dan's recovery. Pooh was always eager and happy to see Dan, to play with him, and to go on walks with him. Theirs was a real love affair that paid great dividends. Any other pet (such as a cat or a bird) would not have stimulated Dan to exercise. And a larger dog would not have been manageable in Dan's weakened condition. Pooh the Pomeranian was the perfect stimulus. Dan returned to 95 percent of his prestroke capabilities within about six months, and then continued to improve afterward.

Over the ensuing years, Dan's health gradually waned, but he remained mentally active and got around pretty well with a cane. Though unsteady on his feet, he actively participated in activities that he loved and enjoyed interactions with others. At ninety-seven-years old, Dan injured himself in a minor fall and needed physical therapy in a rehab center again. While living there, Dan received frequent visits from his friends and, of course, from Jenn and Pooh. One day, as his therapist prepared for his daily morning exercise, Dan's heart gave out, and he passed quickly and easily from this life.

In the spectrum of spiraling capabilities, it really doesn't get much better than this. Dan enjoyed a long, active life interrupted by occasional health issues with relatively short recovery periods. A few key elements of this success story are worth highlighting:

* Active participation, support, and encouragement from his spouse, Jenn, and local family members
* Encouragement from the local community with which he had been actively involved
* Regular exercise and physical stimulation in caring for Pooh, a sweet and manageably sized dog
* Dan's ongoing optimism about aging and rehabilitation and avoidance of self-pity over his eroding and lost capabilities.

But even with this prolonged success story of aging, Dan and Jenn still relied on rehabilitation centers and maintained an awareness of facilities and their reputations. Their research primarily involved paying attention when they visited friends in various facilities. By observing the care they received, Dan and Jenn stayed sufficiently informed to make intelligent decisions when they were needed.

Finding Peace in the Spiral

Jane's mom, Nell, had aged in-place in her home for fifteen years after the death of her husband. Then she had a "small" stroke that resulted in physical changes, loss of speech, and her first stay in a rehabilitation center. But after a few weeks, Nell was back at home, managing a bit less well but still able to get by on her own. Another few weeks later, Nell had a second stroke, a massive one that affected her overall health, taking away her speech, mobility, ability to concentrate, ability to eat on her own, and other capabilities that would never return. This time she was in rehab for one hundred days, the maximum time allowed by Medicare. She needed constant supervision and professional help. Jane moved her into an assisted-living center where Nell could obtain progressive levels of care as they were needed.

From that time on, Jane and her husband had box seats at Nell's dramatic, two-year spiral of lost capabilities. They learned that the first stroke is often just the first in a continuing series of strokes. With Nell's continuing strokes, Jane learned about dementia and atrial fibrillation's impact on clotting. However, even more challenging than learning to define these terms was learning to deal with the ensuing medical conditions. When another massive stroke hijacked more of Nell's functions, she lost the use of her right hand and leg. That meant she could no longer walk, get in and out of bed, or perform personal hygiene of any kind. She could not dress herself or put on shoes. She became incontinent. Though she was able to feed herself with her left, nondominant hand, she cared little for food. And Jane periodically received a call in the wee hours of the morning that Nell had fallen out of bed onto the floor, sometimes completely naked. The therapist often indicated that Nell didn't understand what happened or how.

These physical losses came with equally tragic mental loss. Nell lived in a fog. She could focus only for seconds or minutes of time. Her therapist said that when asked to point to an image of a dog among other animals, Nell could recognize and point to the dog one out of ten times. Only 10 percent! And that might just as likely have been a random choice. Though she had lost her use of speech during an earlier period, Nell had been able to communicate on a limited basis. That ability had now effectively vanished too.

And the last stroke took her smile with it.

It was excruciating to observe this deterioration with no hope of reversal. Two months in rehab working with physical, occupational, and speech therapists yielded no return of Nell's previous abilities. Knowledgeable health-care professionals indicated that she would never get better. She would live out her the rest of her life in the "memory unit" of an assisted-living facility, wearing an adult diaper, pushed in a wheelchair, and sleeping with a guardrail designed to keep children from falling out of their beds. Jane and her husband, Bruce, were certain this tragedy had reached its final act.

Compounding Jane and Bruce's grief and distress was dealing with conflicting medical information and advice.

One doctor advised them to wean Nell off her blood-thinner medicine and let nature take its course. In contrast, the rehab doctor scoffed at the idea of changing her meds. He claimed she would be fine with current meds and the new ones (a larger dose of aspirin) he was prescribing.

Therapists first told them how lovely and wonderful it was to work with Nell, but, when pressed, they told the "real story" of her current reality. Directors of the senior-care facilities made sweeping assurances of their staff's constant supervision and care. Yet, Nell still periodically fell out of bed.

They were left wondering:

"Do we keep her on a blood thinner, avoiding clots that would mean another stroke? But what if a fall causes irreparable internal bleeding? Do we take her off the blood thinner to limit risks of internal bleeding when we know that a stroke is a heartbeat away?

"Should we move her closer to us?"

"Should we get yet another opinion about her medical treatment?"

And after Nell was moved to a "memory unit" that provided more care but at a much-greater expense, with a great deal of guilt Jane and Bruce also wondered, "If she lives indefinitely like this—how will we pay for it?"

To add to the continuously unraveling tragedy, Jane and Bruce were stunned to realize that they couldn't seem to find an answer to the most important question of all: "What's the best way for us to love her?" In this and many other situations, the parent is often not the one who is under stress. It is the caregivers! The parent with diminished capabilities just takes life one moment at a time, appreciating small kindnesses and often maintaining a cheerful countenance. But the caregivers are wondering what's needed, what's best, and how to cope while living the rest of their own lives. So their focus should be on finding affordable and acceptable care for the parent without creating stressful situations for themselves.

Elimination of the caregivers' stress will enable them to have greater empathy for their parents, which will result in greater comfort for the aging parents. A stressed-out caregiver is usually not much help to anyone.

Coping with the Reality of Aging

As illustrated by these anecdotal vignettes spanning years to decades, statistics show that most people end up in some kind of caregiving facility several times and will most likely wind up there for the final stages of their lives. It may be an assisted-living facility, a hospital, a hospice, or some other facility. It may be for only a short time, or it may be an extended period. Nevertheless, it is a highly likely occurrence, whether they desire it or not. That end-of-life phase will be greatly improved for all—the parent under care as well as the caregivers—if it is anticipated and some planning is done, even if it is minimal. Preparation makes a lot of difference in the experience, financially, mentally, and emotionally. As most of our aging parents lose capabilities, they must deal with the losses on a daily basis. They learn to accept them. Or if they don't want to accept them, they may try to delay them through improving their diets and increasing their exercise. But that only delays the experience. It doesn't avoid it. Soon enough, the decline will be encountered once again. For sure, changing diets and exercise routines can substantially improve the quality of life during this phase, but it doesn't change the inevitable. It is simply delayed.

Throughout the extended period of declining capabilities, there are often no simple answers and few sources of real comfort. Humor, kindness, love, patience, genuine concern, and tenderness make the experience easier to accept for the parent. These items and others are termed the fruits of the Spirit by the apostle Paul (Gal. 5:22). For sure, these fruits bring peace to the parent. Cynicism, sarcasm, rudeness, jealousy, envy, and anger don't help in any way and usually cause some kind of strife. Although these are also simply human characteristics, they are to be avoided if at all possible.

But the caregiver is the one searching for solutions and is not guaranteed of finding them. So what is the caregiver to do? The primary solutions that have worked for us are acceptance, preparation, and avoiding generation of inner frustration and bottling up of emotion. After prayer and deliberation, we have embraced the following plan:

* **Kindness and acceptance**: The caregivers agreed to be kind to themselves individually and to others in their relationship. Second-guessing and guilt are intense when it comes to caring for an aging parent. Caregiving at this stage takes its toll on the caregivers—physically, mentally, and especially emotionally. Often even the experts cannot agree on the best course of treatment. There is no cure for old age. There are only stalling and delaying tactics and ways to enhance the

quality of life. For that reason, caregivers should also commit to care for one another and to be kind to themselves (and each other, if there are more than one). They can be of no value to their parents if they are emotionally depleted and guilt-ridden.

* **Talking to experts:** In a continuing search for information relevant to the parents' situation, seek insights and guidance from experts in the physical, mental, emotional, and legal or financial matters associated with the end stages of life. Talk to medical, financial, and end-of-life experts to determine how your parents' quality of life can be improved and what can be anticipated from this point forward.

* **Sharing emotions:** Rather than internalizing and bottling up your own feelings, find useful and accessible outlets to eliminate the pent-up frustrations and irritations associated with not being in control. If unable to tackle the trauma by yourselves, look for support from trusted friends and family. It helps to explain your need for an outlet before beginning this so others will not think you're looking to them for answers. You simply need a relief valve that will have no consequences.

* **Praying:** As a Christian, pray daily for God's wisdom and mercy. This is another relief valve that has proven to work remarkably well.

These steps brought a significant degree of peace to us, despite many frustrating situations over which we had no control. Acceptance and peace will enable you to better understand and deal with the myriad of caregiving situations throughout the expected extended time it will be encountered.

There is no cure for old age.
Accept that fact. Be kind
and patient. Avoid hostilities whenever possible.
The resulting journey will be
more pleasant for all.

Maintaining the Will to Live

Passing on a Legacy

As we near the end of this book, we must begin thinking about the end—of our parents' lives and of our journey as caregivers. When bodies are healthy, minds are still sharp, and friends and family are vibrant and fun, no one really wants to think about the end. However, after a spouse dies or friends of the same age pass on, the simple pleasures of life seem to diminish, with fewer people to share the remaining joys. These facts of an aging life make it harder to find the motivation to live.

Our parents may begin to take a fatalistic attitude, and it can be easy for us to be dismissive: "Oh Dad, put those thoughts out of your mind!" "Mom, don't be so pessimistic. Life is still good. We're here to take care of you, and you know you enjoy the grandkids when they're around." In reality, our parents are coming to grips with their mortality and realizing that their time is limited. That certainly doesn't mean they're abandoning all joy and satisfaction in life. On the contrary, aging people have many end-of-life pleasures to enjoy.

The company of loved ones, like children and grandchildren, remains a primary source of pleasure and joy. Seniors almost always delight in sharing their life stories with those who are interested, whether family, friends, or even strangers. But many other pleasures can also generate a renewed sense of purpose and desire to live.

* **Establishing financial security for their progeny.** Seniors can be extremely motivated by building a trust or

custodial account to enhance the lives of their adult children and grandchildren. Funds could be established toward a college education, a car, a house, or any other reason. But this type of project often gives our parents a tangible, ongoing goal. They may even enjoy working with children and grandchildren, depending on common interests and capabilities. Together, they could assess investment options, make the necessary decisions, carry them out, track progress, and adapt as needed over time.

* **Passing the baton of lifelong passions to the next generation.** Similarly, passing the baton for a shared passion can also create a strong sense of purpose for our parents. Some examples are environmental concerns or preservation of our national parks heritage. They can research their interests, identify worthwhile causes, follow their progress, and find ways to serve. They can also teach, mentor, or collaborate with like-minded younger people. Lifelong passions for careers, hobbies, politics, religion, and communities often cross generational lines, so old and young can work together to promote and galvanize their shared vision. Accomplishing short-term goals together creates camaraderie and immediate satisfaction. The long-term impact can often be substantial for our parents, while simultaneously improving and enriching the world around us.

* **Deepening perspectives on history for younger generations.** Many of our parents possess priceless, personal perspective about historical events and the underpinnings of our way of life. In sharing their experiences, they ensure that younger generations hear and consider the important stories that are the foundation of much of our culture. For example, survivors of the World War II attack on Pearl Harbor

recount their stories daily to spellbound audiences visiting the memorial of that event in Hawaii. Many veterans serve as staff members for national memorials without remuneration. Opportunities for this type of direct contribution of knowledge abound—at any memorial or museum nationwide, community events, schools, churches, celebratory functions, reunions, and more. Again, finding ways to share their experiences can give seniors a deep sense of purpose and fulfillment while inspiring and equipping the next generation.

* **Caring for those in need.** Our parents often find purpose and meaning in helping others who are in some sort of significant need. Countless organizations devote themselves to helping others and depend on volunteers to thrive—civic clubs like Kiwanis or Elks; medical foundations like St. Jude's hospital; and both local and national organizations like the Salvation Army, Meals on Wheels, Alzheimer's Foundation, or Wounded Warrior Foundation. These vast opportunities add dimension and purpose to the lives of their supporters that is hard to quantify but impossible to overlook.

Long-term goals and purpose make it easier for our parents (as well as other seniors or anyone else) to stay motivated in life and maintain a positive attitude. The simple act of helping others stimulates the helper in ways that are difficult to describe, but the impact is hard to ignore. It takes our minds off our own troubles and fills the empty space inside us when we are drifting and lonely. One of the hardest things about aging, especially into the eighties and nineties, is losing long-term companions, whether family or friends. Those losses create a vacuum that is difficult to fill with new and emerging relationships. But grief can also make us more sensitive and compassionate to the plights of others. As a result, it often also stimulates new interests and objectives. Find ways to gently encourage your parents to maintain their sense of purpose, help others, look for joy, and keep a sense of humor, even as they face the pain of loss.

Coming to grips with mortality and a limited amount of remaining time doesn't mean abandoning joy and a fulfilling life.

Staying Healthy to the End?

In his early nineties but still active and alert, Ken loved to eat at his favorite German restaurant once or twice a month. But since he had recently been diagnosed with a mild form of diabetes, he had to watch his diet more closely than he desired. His much-younger wife often reminded him of his restrictions. But on one occasion, when his son and family were visiting from out of town for Ken's birthday, he decided he wanted a dark German beer.

His wife chimed in, "Ken, you'd better watch your diet. That's richer than you should have."

With a twinkle in his eye, his immediate comeback was, "What's it going to do? Shorten my lifespan?" Despite his health-based restrictions, he still maintained his zest for life, enjoyed his family, and occasionally indulged in favorite pleasures to the end.

Keeping a Lively Sense of Humor

When Mike was helping his mother Clarice get her affairs in order, they eventually got around to discussing her funeral services. He was copiously taking notes about burial locations, pallbearers, officiates, and her other preferences. Since Clarice was a dedicated Christian who had always attended church regularly and loved to sing, he asked her what hymns she would like sung at the service. As he continued to take notes, her answer left him speechless and laughing. "Surprise me!" she said. Clarice was clearly prepared for the end, while still enjoying a rich sense of humor. Hopefully, we can all maintain a similar attitude for a long time.

Hanging On

Nora's son Claude lived in another state, about a day's drive away. But Claude traveled on business on a monthly basis to the area where Nora and her husband lived. She had been homebound for several years due to a slip on ice that cracked her hip, which never completely healed. Being homebound and in another state, Nora no longer visited much with Claude or her grandchildren. With little family interaction and no purpose, she slowly withered away. Because of her condition, her doctor recommended that she be placed under hospital care to assure that she got enough nourishment and attention.

On one of Claude's monthly trips, he visited with her every day in the hospital—chatting, reliving memories, and showing her recent photographs of his kids. Each time he came, it brought a smile to her gaunt face. The day he planned to leave and go home, she took a turn for the worse, so Claude decided to make an extra visit as he left town. When he arrived, the nurse told him that Nora was not conscious, but he went to her room anyway. He sat quietly with her for a while. When he was ready to go, he said, "Bye for now, Mom," and stroked her hair.

His voice and his touch aroused something inside her. Without opening her eyes, she raised up and quietly said, "Claude!"

Surprised, he stopped, and caressed her head gently again. Then her whole body relaxed and sagged back onto the bed, and she passed away shortly afterward. Though her psyche had given up her will to live, she hung onto life long enough to say one last good-bye. This is a fairly common occurrence. Our quiet presence can be a final comfort to our loved ones near death. Even if they do not appear to be responsive, take the time to share your love with invalid parents when the opportunity arises.

Calling Roll

After suffering from Alzheimer's for about a decade, Bev didn't know there was anything wrong with her. She was happy and content in a way that's typical for Alzheimer's patients. Bev's contentment frequently turned into real joy whenever she sang. She loved to sing her favorite church hymns—usually at the top of her melodic voice. Near the end of her life, she often sang "When the Roll Is Called up Yonder." The ending of this hymn is in the last part of the chorus, "When the roll is called up yonder, I'll be there!"

When Bev sang this favorite hymn, she always concluded after the chorus, "And I will! I'll be there! You wait and see."

Her faith and confidence brought joy to many others with her happy declaration. If only we could all live our lives that way each day—with such contentment, peace, and joy.

Carrying on through Thick and Thin

Many excellent works discuss the challenge of maintaining a will to live. Though we are certainly not philosophers, our favorite book about this topic is Viktor Frankl's classic, *Man's Search for Meaning*. In this work, Frankl draws from personal experience during the World War II Holocaust to describe how an overriding purpose can sustain someone in spite of horrendous living conditions. In applying these lessons to our caregiving situation, we see that finding a meaningful and sustainable purpose is a key challenge for both caregivers and their parents. Once we identify and accept a viable purpose, we have a reason to get up and get engaged every day.

Abraham Maslow, in his classic *Hierarchy of Needs*, also discusses the overriding purpose, but only after first addressing the individual's need for intimacy and love. That fits with our caregiving experiences too. Our aging parents crave growing and meaningful relationships with family and friends. In Maslow's hierarchy, that need arises immediately after basic physiological and safety needs are fulfilled. When we experience love and intimacy, we can begin to consider purpose.

**Helping your parents find a purpose
can be the stimulus to make the
best of what they have for as
long as they have it.**

In summary, the will to live is a highly individual trait. If someone doesn't have it, there is little we can do that will make a difference. For sure, our lecturing and sermonizing will make no impact. When our parents decide that their "time has come," the best thing we can do is to show them loving attention: touching, listening, affirming, sharing, and often just sitting quietly with them, holding hands. The will to live may be rekindled. But even if it is not, we have provided them love and comfort to the end.

Preparing for the Inevitable: When Life Ends

by Bruce Black

Author's Note: This section takes a decidedly different approach than the previous sections since one of the authors is a minister. Having dealt with the end of life throughout his career, he has a unique perspective on this issue, gleaned from a lifetime of counseling sessions and eulogies.

A Lifetime of Eulogies

My role as a minister over twenty-five years has provided scores of opportunities to work with families dealing with death. Most of those experiences have been associated with the loss of an older parent or spouse. A family member or a funeral-home director usually contacts me to ask if I will perform the service of their now-deceased loved one.

Early in my career, I developed the habit of meeting the family in their home or in a comfortable setting prior to the funeral so that I can gain information and insight about the deceased. During this meeting, I cover the specifics of the funeral service and ask for any additional requests. But the real reason for the meeting is to help the family open up and express their emotions and memories connected to the person we will be honoring at the funeral. These information-gathering sessions typically take place around the family's dining-room table and last between one-and-a-half to three hours. After exchanging some informal introductions and some small talk, we sit down, and I take out my laptop for notes. Then I lead the family through a host of questions about the deceased:

* Where was he or she born?
* What were his or her parents' names, and what did they do for a living?
* Where did he or she live while growing up?
* Where did he or she go to school?
* How many siblings did he or she have, and how many are still living?
* What were his or her hobbies growing up?
* Did he or she go to college?
* When did he or she move away from home?
* When and where did he or she meet his or her spouse?
* What did he or she do for a living?
* When and where were their children born? What were the circumstances?
* What were your favorite memories of your mom or dad?
* What did your parent or spouse do for fun?
* Who were his or her friends and what were those relationships like?
* Tell me about your husband's or wife's work life.
* What were his or her defining character traits? Where did those originate?
* What is something that people admired about him or her?
* What was it you loved most about your spouse?

I learned a long time ago that though I asked for these meetings to help me prepare a personal funeral talk, something far more important was happening at the dining-room table. The surviving family members find deep comfort and even joy as they share their memories. During these sessions that were supposedly held to help me be more effective, families are drawn closer to one another as they share laughter and tears by remembering the loved one they have just lost. As the "outsider," I am always humbled and uplifted by these sessions. I've learned from these meetings that curiosity and compassion go together. Answering questions about a lost loved one arouses deep compassion in the family members for the individual who is gone.

Preparing while Still Alive-the Personal Touch

I'm convinced there's a lesson from these experiences for those of us whose parents are still living. I need to become more inquisitive about my own parents too. As I am now entering the ranks of senior citizenship myself, I face the temptation of believing that I know everything about my eighty-plus-year-old parents. But I don't. There are simple things I still don't know about my mom and dad, even at my age. For example:

* I don't know where my mother went to elementary school.
* Who was her best childhood friend?
* What did it feel like for my father to grow up in the home of an alcoholic?
* What did my mother and her sister do for fun growing up during the Great Depression?
* What it was like being a teenager living through World War II?

I have a host of questions about my own parents that I want answered. I want to turn toward my parents with the same curiosity that I developed through helping other families make funeral preparations. I want to learn more about them while they are still with me. I want to experience the joys and comfort of recounting their lives and sharing memories with them while they are still living. Because if I do, I believe it will deepen my love for them.

I envision this starting simply—something like, "Hey Mom, I just finished reading a great book about people living in your generation. I was wondering, what was it like for you growing up in your family during the Depression? What did you do for fun when resources were so limited?"

Knowing my mom, I believe she will answer me quickly. Her response will cause me to think of any number of follow-up questions. Then I will use these questions to create a continuing dialogue with her for more information about her childhood and early adulthood, thereby enlightening me and helping us grow closer together while she is still here.

I suspect that since reliving our parents' lives after they are gone brings great comfort, joy, and compassion, then reliving our parents' lives while they are still alive will bring the same or even greater comfort, joy, and compassion. I suspect that the more we know about them, the deeper our love will be for them. As we engage our curiosity about our parents today as adults, we are better able to understand their situations, challenges, decisions, joys, frustrations, and disappointments. As mature adults, we have been through some of those experiences ourselves, so we will be more compassionate than we ever could have imagined when we were younger and less sensitive. I plan to increase my compassion quotient (if there is such a thing) toward my parents.

**Don't wait to make your relationship
a lasting and really personal one.
When your parents are gone, it's
too late. Have no regrets.**

If you've already lost a parent, you can still use this link of curiosity and compassion. Get your family together for the purpose of sharing memories about your deceased parent(s). Plan for this time during family get-togethers, on holidays, or on the anniversary of their birthdays. As the group shares memories of your loved one, listen carefully. Pay attention to the emotions you experience. My guess is that you will not only learn things about your parent(s) that you didn't know or have slipped from your memory but that you will also find a comfort and peace and deeper love wash over you.

Preparing while Still Alive-the Administrative Necessities

As I work with many grieving families struggling to put together final arrangements for a deceased parent or spouse, I often see capable, successful, loving and articulate people at a loss for words and unable to act. With longing and emotional stares, they ask:

* What do you think I should do?
* What would my father want?
* I have no idea what his or her wishes were. Cremation? Burial? Where?
* What would he or she want at his or her funeral?
* Do you have a funeral home that you can recommend?

Since most of us go through this process only a few times in our lives, we find ourselves in unfamiliar territory and want to be told what to do. Especially in our time of grief, we want someone else to make the hard decisions. A survey published online on Yahoo on May 6, 2012 from RocketLawyer.com gives these startling statistics:[11]

---

11 finance.yahoo.com/blogs/the-exchange/half-americans-set-die-without-193140015. html

* Fifty percent of Americans with children will die without a will.
* Forty-one percent of baby boomers aged fifty-five to sixty-four don't have a will.
* The top three reasons cited by survey respondents for not having a will are
  1) procrastination;
  2) belief that they don't need one; and
  3) cost.

We can assume that if most adults don't have wills, then they certainly haven't talked to their children or spouses about funeral details. Both of these realities present daunting challenges to the family that remains behind.

Let's put the shoe on the other foot for a moment and consider your own funeral. What do you feel? Is it an overwhelming sense of calm as you realize that you have addressed the reality of your death and have made appropriate plans? Or does the thought of dying cause your chest to tighten, your pulse to quicken, and your hands to show a slight tremor? If you have a tough time facing and preparing for the inevitable in your own life, then you can be pretty confident that your parents feel the same way. Furthermore, as we just read, if your parents are baby boomers, there is a 59 percent chance that they haven't faced the reality of their death, much less put together their funeral and burial plans.

Considering the fact that most Americans are in denial about growing older (much less dying), the question facing adult children is: What can we do to ensure that we are ready and prepared for our parents' deaths, funerals, and burials? How can we determine our parents' wishes for their "final arrangements" so we can be sure to carry them out? Here's a suggested starting point. Make your own final arrangements. That's right! Make your own arrangements first. Meet with a lawyer or go to an online legal service and get the following legal documents to ensure you have them for yourself and your spouse:

* A durable power of attorney (financial directive)
* A living will (health-care directive)
* A will
* A trust

Go online or talk to a lawyer to gain more insight about the purpose and usefulness of each of these items. While working to put these documents together for your own life, begin thinking about your own funeral. Write down your wishes for your own funeral and burial arrangements:

* What do you want done with your body? Burial? Cremation?
* What funeral home do you wish to use?
* Do you want a funeral service? A memorial service? A grave-side ceremony?
* Who would you like to speak at your funeral?
* What music would you like performed?
* Is there anything you would like read or shared?
* If you want to be buried, who should carry the casket to the grave (pallbearers)?
* Would you like your family to gather for a meal afterward?

For example, here are my own wishes for my funeral and burial. I want to be cremated as cheaply as possible through a local crematorium.

I want my ashes to be scattered. (My grandfather had a friend who said he wanted his ashes to be taken to the local Walmart. That way, he knew his wife would see him at least twice a day!) Seriously, the reason I wish to be cremated is that it takes away a lot of decisions that my family will have to make at the time of my death. They will not have to decide about body preparation, clothing choices, burial plots and maintenance arrangements, and overall cost. (The average cost of a funeral in the United States is now sixty-six hundred dollars. Plan to add an additional three thousand dollars if you wish to be buried in a cemetery. By contrast, cremation costs about fifteen hundred dollars or less. Since I am not a big spender, I believe in our old family mottos: Anyone can pay retail! So I always look for a wholesale (or cheap) solution. They also will not have to go through the ordeal of viewing my remains. I have chosen to have my ashes scattered so they will not feel like they have to return to a graveyard to pay their respects to me.

I want my funeral to be a time of reunion and as much fun as possible with memories shared by my family and friends. I would like the song "Don't You Forget About Me" by Simple Minds to be played. (Remember the movie *The Breakfast Club*?) I want my friends and family to share memories of good times that they had with me. I want a few tears to be shed too, so the minister of our church can tell stories of how I will be missed. I want my family and friends to eat together after my funeral. Anyone who knows me knows I love to go out to eat. I especially love eating at restaurants with my wife and kids while using a discount coupon. (Remember: anyone can pay retail!) For a meal following my burial, I would like my family to do the same (using a discount coupon), preferably at a Red Lobster or Olive Garden. (I have always loved their cheese biscuits and breadsticks respectively).

That is enough about my funeral. Yours will be different. However, addressing the major questions I've raised here is critical. Having a plan will be a great blessing to your remaining family. Now back to finding out about your parents' final wishes...

Making your own funeral arrangements now will be a blessing to your kids. It also gives you credibility to bring up the subject with your parents.

And Now...?

Once you have completed the work for your own passing by assembling your durable power of attorney, living will, will, and living trust and have also written down your wishes for your final arrangements, you are ready to contact your parents. Send a copy of these items to your parents with this statement: "Here are my (our) arrangements. It was more complex and required more thought than I had anticipated. Can we talk about your plans? When can we get together to do this?" Once you have paved the way in your own life by getting these important decisions and documents prepared, your parents may find it easier to follow you down the path. Since you already have been down this path before them, you have more credibility. You can help them work through their own personal anxiety much easier once you have worked through your own. You can refer them to websites, lawyers, funeral homes, or ministers that helped you in making sure your family was prepared to carry out your wishes.

As our parents taught us, "Lead by example." Not only that, you have just given your own children and family the great blessing of sharing your final wishes.

Chapter 6

Reflections-Looking in the Rearview Mirror

Was It Worth It? Would We Do It Again?

In the romantic drama *Hope Floats*, the female lead, Birdee Pruitt, makes this observation to her daughter in a difficult discussion about life,

> "Beginnings are scary, endings are usually sad, but it's the middle that counts the most. Try to remember that when you find yourself at a new beginning. Just give hope a chance to float up. And it will too."

That certainly is true to our experience, whether it's a new job, a relocation, a new relationship, or even a new life phase—like taking care of aging parents. When we started the caregiving phase of life, we felt scared and overwhelmed. And the ending? Well, we already knew that outcome—for everyone! Just like Birdee explained, endings are usually sad. As for the middle, we would do many things differently if given the chance: better preparation, more patience, and a greater focus on enhancing the relationships, among many others. But in answer to the questions posed here, was it worth it, and would we do it again? We would answer both questions with a resounding, "Yes!" Our relationships with our parents grew closer and more meaningful.

So many little things made big differences in their daily lives. That in itself was rewarding, more so than we ever expected. Furthermore, we learned patience and gentleness (at least to a greater degree than before) in helping them deal with their own challenges. In summary, we really did grow up as they grew old, just like the subtitle of this book suggests. That process happened through experiences and attitudes that resulted in unexpected changes in ourselves while simultaneously providing needed support to those we love.

This is a phase of life that most of us do not prepare for sufficiently, if at all. This is a wonderful way to do something meaningful and lasting with "the middle" of life, just as Birdee Pruitt emphasized. In showing concern, just by reading this book, you're already ahead of the game and on the way to unanticipated blessings. Even so, consider the contrast with becoming a new parent for the first time.

When new parents bring home their first child, there is usually joy and happiness written all over their faces. But despite their joy, they are also exhausted. How can that tiny human being demand so much emotional and physical energy? Most parents find out they are expecting with many months to prepare and launch into an eager quest to discover all they can about nurturing a baby.

That's why the book *What to Expect When You Are Expecting* has topped bestseller lists for several decades. The reason for the book's success is obvious. First-time mothers and fathers recognize the need for expert help and counsel as they prepare to face one of life's most rewarding, yet sobering, experiences—having a baby. They crave data and wisdom from experts as well as from parents they admire. They seek out detailed explanations of the biological, emotional, and practical intricacies of the human gestation process. They heed recommendations for sleep, diet, vitamin intake, exercise, and doctor selection. Especially if they live far from family and have not yet closely observed the child-bearing process, this book can become like a Bible for first-time parents. Fortunately, it doesn't take much discernment to recognize that the child is on the way so you can start planning. A simple, two-minute test is all you need to get started.

If only planning for aging parents was that straightforward and unequivocal. Wouldn't it be great if we could just give Mom and Dad a quick "aging" test from the local pharmacy? Afterward, we could pick up a book to help us track the rate and scope of their physical, mental, and emotional decline. Alas, it doesn't work that way. In stark contrast to the aggressive pursuit of information on growing babies, most adult children do the exact opposite when dealing with aging parents. When first confronted with the signs, most people lean toward "aggressive avoidance" as their primary strategy.

As we've seen in many of the vignettes throughout the earlier sections, denial can make the reality pretty devastating. What's worse is that nothing can be done to stop it. Aging never reverses.

We just keep getting older every single day. The challenges keep coming, and they are usually compounded with other complications.

Why is this so disconcerting? For many of us, the true heroes of our lives are our mom and dad. Though certainly flawed, they had a greater impact on our development than anyone else in our lives. They often provided stability from the moment we drew our first breaths and have continued to do so throughout our lifetimes. Decades later, we must face the reality that their capabilities are ebbing away and that they will die, sooner than we want. This reality can be overwhelming.

Understandably, our parents don't want to face this unpleasant and fearful reality either. Even if they do, the diminishing effects of the aging process may not fully register with them. Add to the typical denials by both parents and adult children the fact that many of our parents believe that asking for help, especially from our children, is seen as a sign of selfishness and weakness.

So we don't want to deal with the diminishing capacity of our parents. Our parents don't want to admit it, may not notice it, and won't readily ask for our help. Yet none of this changes the reality.

**Our parents have lived long enough
to need our care and help.
We are tasked and called to honor
them and take care of them.**

As we close this book, we reflect on our full experience, the countless stories we've heard from others, and the myriad circumstances.

We have lived and observed the benefits arising from honoring our aging parents. Some of these became obvious in the middle of the process. But most of the benefits are only noticed in hindsight.

That really shouldn't be a surprise, should it? When preparing for a career, we study material that appeared to be unrelated and unfulfilling. Only after we have a chance to apply it, often years later, does its value become clear. Similarly, in training for athletic competition, we train and practice until our skills become somewhat automatic, and we are as ready as possible for game day. In each of those situations, hindsight reveals that preparation was the key to success, often accompanied by a bit of luck. But the preparation and the realization of its purpose are often years apart. Additionally, we could not have identified the right preparation without guidance. Instead, a teacher or a coach with wisdom and experience helped us to prepare.

In contrast, when preparing to care for aging parents, the needs usually become obvious *before* the preparation. So we are often shocked and dismayed by our unexpected yet clear incompetency. That is what makes the responsibility so daunting. We see the big picture of what needs to be accomplished and addressed without seeing all the elements of the solution. However, we can draw one important parallel between honoring aging parents and preparing for a career or an athletic event: we usually recognize the value of our herculean efforts only in hindsight.

**After our parents are gone, we see
the most obvious benefit to
our labors: a closer relationship with our parents.**

Just as parents bond with their children in helping them to mature, grown children bond with their parents in helping them weather their natural decline. This was not expected. We thought we knew our parents. But after helping them with downsizing, financial challenges, physical functions, appointments, and countless other tasks of daily living, we now see that there were many aspects of their lives that we knew nothing about. And through countless discussions with them during this process, we learned more about the lifestyles, choices, and experiences spanning their lifetimes. Honoring and caring for our aging parents gave us a greater appreciation of them as individuals than we ever had before. But even now, years later, we still regularly ponder, "Why did they do that?" Or we stumble upon photographs and letters, and wonder, "Who was that person? It's obvious that they were important, but I don't have a clue who they are."

**We derived a great deal of comfort
and satisfaction from having
supported our parents and easing their
burden throughout their aging.**

In the Bible, the wise king Solomon wrote, "Children's children are a crown to the aged and parents are the pride of their children." (Prov. 17:6) That may not seem possible in the middle of a spat over some current issue, but, again, in time, we find that we remember fondly those things that we most admired in our parents, even the grumpier ones. In hindsight, we often forgive the grumbling and recall events with affection, humor, and poignancy.

Reconciliation and Resolution

It was a touching scene. Martha's daughter Jill, now in her early sixties, sat down on the side of the hospital bed that swaddled her mother. She knew that her mother was likely in the final hours of her life. Martha was attached to a myriad of monitors and tubes. She had pneumonia, and infection raced through her body. Her ability to speak left her long ago. The doctors were unsure of her recovery. As Jill sat by her mother's side, she brushed her mother's hair out of her eyes, unsure if Martha even recognized her. Then, teary-eyed, Jill said, "Mom, I really do love you." Seconds later, she added, "Mom, I hope you can forgive me." Still intently staring into her mother's face a few minutes later she whispered, "Mom, I forgive you for everything."

Trust us when we tell you that conflict with parents never goes away by itself. Unresolved, it lasts until the end of life. But that is painful and makes any caregiving efforts harder than they already are. Although sometimes parents will not allow reconciliation, as far as it depends on you, work to find resolution, and do so earlier rather than later in life. As difficult as it may seem to be, face up to conflict as quickly as it appears. Work toward full, two-way reconciliation, with both yourself and your parent participating actively. But if that is not possible, resolve both to seek and to give forgiveness to attain as much resolution as possible. The sadness and regrets from not doing so are hard to overcome at the end of life as the moments ebb away.

Reconcile differences before it's too late.

Final Thoughts

In a final reflection on the long process of caring for our aging parents, here are a few simple and overarching lessons we have learned:

* **Don't wait to address unresolved conflict with your parents.** Unaddressed problems often intensify and metastasize with time. Find the courage to speak up, address the issues, and find the humility and patience to repair any relational damage. For Christians, the Bible clearly states that honoring your parents is God's idea, but resolving conflicts also makes caring for them much easier and more fulfilling.

* **Don't wait to start talking with your parents about aging.** Do more than joke with your parents about aging and "senior moments." This may be a convenient way to broach a taboo topic, but don't simply tease about it. Instead, look for ways to start this needed and serious conversation. Humor may be part of it, but watch for other opportunities—like a funeral, life transitions, the decline of their friends, and increasing complaints of aches and pains. Talk to them about their expectations and desires as they age. Don't put it off. Just do it! And start now!

* **Don't wait to become educated.** You've already started the process by reading this book. Good for you! That's a lot more than most people do and hopefully it has been timely too. When a crisis arises, you'll already know something about the aging process physically, mentally, and emotionally. Keep learning. Listen more carefully to people who are already actively caring for their parents. Question them about their approaches and their successes and failures. Ask for their insights. You'll learn a lot. Most of us want to

share experiences and reflect on them. When you stumble upon an article about aging, stop and actually read it rather than put it aside to read it later, "when you have time." We discovered many of these articles in our files months or years after it was too late. When you notice your parents struggling, gently probe them. As their decline progresses, engage the challenges instead of avoiding them. Look up "aging parents" on your search engine. Find help. Attend seminars. Listen to podcasts. Read books. Join a caregivers' support group. Do these things before a crisis, if possible, while you still have time to prepare, make choices, and take action. Though circumstances are vastly different, there is a typical set of experiences that most aging parents and their caregivers encounter. Understanding the process will help prepare you to support your parents in their time of need.

Caring for your aging parents can be a tremendous challenge, yet it can also be a sweet and tender opportunity. Being informed, equipped, and emotionally prepared can help turn one of life's most formidable trials into one of its most fulfilling joys.

You're Next! Are You Ready for Your Own Aging?

Benjamin Franklin once wrote, "but in this world nothing can be said to be certain, except death and taxes." If Ben were alive today, he might more appropriately say, "but in this world nothing can be said to be certain, except for death, taxes, and aging."

No matter the advances in health care, drug discovery, or selective surgery, aging is a reality. Time marches on and affects our lives. This book was primarily written to help future caregivers gain new awareness about our aging parents so that we can emotionally prepare and support them. Hopefully after reading this book you can avoid some of the mistakes we made ourselves. But an ancillary question also needs to be asked: Are you ready to age?

We've already discussed how many of the major complications and frustrations in dealing with aging parents could be eliminated or at least minimized by earlier conversations and planning. That raises the obvious next question: How can we, as parents, be intentional with our own children? What if we planned not just for funeral and burial expenses but for our own deteriorating capabilities as we age? "But wait," you may say. "You're being too pessimistic. I eat healthy. I exercise. I don't smoke or do crazy things. I don't need an aging plan or strategy!" And there are certainly plenty of self-help books that offer strategies for delaying the effects of aging. "Seventy is the new fifty!" you say, or "Eighty is the new sixty!" That may all very well be true. In fact, many people in active adult communities live like they are half their age with healthy, vibrant lives full of worthy activities and diversions. But vibrant life will not last forever. Eventually, we will slow down, losing speed, reflexes, strength, nimbleness, and endurance. We will encounter "senior moments" and wonder if it is the beginning of dementia or Alzheimer's. Most of us will wonder sometime, if not often, if our financial resources will last as long as we do.

**Start discussing your own aging
with those who will miss you
when you're gone and will feel responsible
when you are no longer independent.
That's time and effort well spent—for all!**

If you are reading this book, your parents probably didn't provide you with many plans for their aging process. Now that you have become aware of the impact and challenges, have you made an aging plan for yourself? How can you make your children's lives a little simpler and their caregiving days a little less stressful?

While there is time—while you are healthy and can do some of your own research and can seek out your own counsel—start planning for your transition from independence to dependence as you age. The more you consider it, plan for it, and talk about it, the more comfortable you will be with the realities of growing older. The negative "vibes" of growing old will soften. Your children will find comfort in knowing your hopes for your future. Here's a good place to start. Do your children know:

* Your desires when you can no longer live in your current house?
* What modifications do you want made to your house to make it age-accessible and prolong your independence a little longer?
* When it will be time for them to help you find another place to live?
* If you currently have trouble hearing the phone ring?

* If your sight causes you to feel insecure or unsafe?
* How you expect to handle basic chores like housecleaning and cooking when those tasks become unmanageable?
* When they should take away your car keys?
* What your overall and specific health issues are?
* Who provides your current and future health-care program?
* Your end-of-life desires?
* Where to find copies of your will or living trusts? Your medical directives? Your durable power of attorney?
* Your financial situation?
* When and where to pay your current and future bills or how to prioritize their payment?
* If your retirement income is directly deposited into your bank account?
* When and how to use a durable power of attorney if needed to manage your finances and make decisions about your health care?
* Who you want to be the executor of your estate?
* Who to contact and what to do in the event of your death?

Aging, like death and taxes, is a subject we love to avoid and try hard to deny. Yet if you are reading this book, you probably already know something about the pain, frustration, and expense that denial and avoidance will bring. Learn from your experience, and find the motivation and strength to answer the questions. Then give your adult children a great gift. Invite them over, sit down, and talk to them about your wishes and plans for growing old. Share with them your desires, and welcome them into the discussion. Be gracious. Be humble. Be prepared to speak but also to listen. Remember, they will likely be the ones carrying out large portions of your aging plans and absorbing the greatest impact of the process.

Recently some friends, a retired couple, both of whom are sixty-four years old, e-mailed their two children, both in their forties. The e-mail carried two attachments and a link—medical directions for each of the parents and contact information for the couple's financial advisor. Most likely, the adult children receiving that e-mail didn't open the medical directives with glee and excitement, if they opened them at all. Yet, those of us who have dealt with aging parents can tell those fortyish adult children that in twenty years they will be thankful for that e-mail, especially if one of their parents is facing a prolonged battle with a debilitating disease that has no cure. Further, the connection to the financial planner implies that the mom and dad have done some planning and preparation for aging. That, too, will be an immeasurable gift for their children.

The reality is this: aging is already upon us. But aging to the point of impacting your independence is probably still somewhere on the horizon. Get ahead of the aging process by starting now.

Fight the tendency to deny the realities of aging and losing your independence. Think through your desires for your place to live, your care and feeding, your health care, and your finances. Then, most importantly, communicate those desires to your adult children. These conversations will enhance your relationship with your children and turn a taboo topic into a time of shared thanksgiving. Life is a struggle. That's not going to change. Embrace it. Then, as the sports announcers say, we can experience the thrill of victory and the agony of defeat. With the right attitude and some preparation, you can count on many more victories than defeats.